Aiming for Progress in
Reading

Book 4
Second Edition

William Collins' dream of knowledge for all began with the publication of his first book in 1819. A self-educated mill worker, he not only enriched millions of lives, but also founded a flourishing publishing house. Today, staying true to this spirit, Collins books are packed with inspiration, innovation and practical expertise. They place you at the centre of a world of possibility and give you exactly what you need to explore it.

Collins. Freedom to teach.

Published by Collins
An imprint of HarperCollins*Publishers*
The News Building
1 London Bridge Street
London SE1 9GF

Browse the complete Collins catalogue at
www.collins.co.uk

© HarperCollins*Publishers* Limited 2014

10 9 8 7 6 5 4 3
ISBN 978-0-00-754747-0

Caroline Bentley-Davies, Gareth Calway, Nicola Copitch, Steve Eddy, Najoud Ensaff, Mike Gould and Mattew Tett assert their moral rights to be identified as the authors of this work.

British Library Cataloguing in Publication Data
A Catalogue record for this publication is available from the British Library.

Commissioned by Catherine Martin
Project managed by Alice Harman
Series Editors Gareth Calway and Mike Gould
Edited in-house by Alicia Higgins
Proofread by Kelly Davis
Designed by Joerg Hartmannsgruber
Typeset by G Brasnett, Cambridge
Cover design by Angela English
Printed and bound by CPI Group (UK) Ltd, Croydon, CR0 4YY

With thanks to Jackie Newman.

Packaged for HarperCollins by
White-Thomson Publishing Ltd.
www.wtpub.co.uk
+44 (0) 843 208 7460

Acknowledgements
The publishers gratefully acknowledge the permissions granted to reproduce copyright material in this book. While every effort has been made to trace and contact copyright holders, where this has not been possible the publishers will be pleased to make the necessary arrangements at the first opportunity.

Extract from *The First Four Minutes* by Sir Roger Bannister, Sutton Publishing. Reprinted with permission of The History Press (p 6); extract from *Screw It, Let's Do It Expanded* by Richard Branson, Virgin Books. Reprinted with permission of The Random House Group Limited (p 7); extract from 'Preludes' by T. S. Eliot, published by Faber & Faber (p 8); extract from 'Friday Night at the Royal Station Hotel' by Philip Larkin in *High Windows*, published by Faber & Faber (p 9); headline 'First the snow, now the ice' by David Brown, *The Times*, © News Syndication 2009 (p 10); 'Snowbound Britain', Gordon Rayner, *Daily Telegraph*, 2 February 2009, The Telegraph Group (pp 10–11); extract from www.specialistmorocco.com Reprinted with permission (p 12); 'Refugee Blues' by W.H Auden (p 16); 'Early Bird Blues' from *Hero and the Girl Next Door* by Sophie Hannah, Carcanet Press. Reprinted with permission of Carcanet Press Ltd (p 16); 'Symptoms' from *Hero and the Girl Next Door* by Sophie Hannah, Carcanet Press. Reprinted with permission of Carcanet Press Ltd (p 18); extracts from *Stone Cold* by Robert Swindells, published by Hamish Hamilton 1993. Text copyright © Robert Swindells 1993. Reprinted with permission of Penguin Books UK (pp 20–21); extracts from 'The Boys Toilets' by Robert Westall, from *Ghost Stories*, Robert Westall, Kingfisher 2004. Reprinted with permission of Laura Cecil Literary Agency (pp 22–23); extracts from *Nothing to be Afraid of* by Jan Mark, Puffin Books. Reprinted with permission of David Higham Associates Ltd (pp 24–25); from 'The Hour and the Man' by Robert Barr (p 28); from 'The

Secret of City Cemetery' by Patrick Bone. Copyright © 1994 by Patrick Bone, first published in Bruce Coville's *Book of Ghosts* (Scholastic Inc 1994) (p 28); from 'The Davenport' by Jack Ritchie. First published in *A Chilling Collection*, edited by Helen Hoke, Dent 1980. Larry Sternig/Jack Byrne Literary Agency (p 29); from 'The Talking Head' by Robert Scott, first published in Dennis Pepper (ed) *The Young Oxford Book of Nasty Endings*, Copyright © Robert Scott 1997. Reprinted here with the author's permission (p 29); from 'Rendevouz' by Daniel Ransome, first published in *Splinters*, ed by R. Baines (p 29); extract from an article in Daily Mail © Daily Mail 2013 (p 30); from *Dreams of Anne Frank* by Bernard Kops, published by Bloomsbury. Reprinted with permission of the publishers (pp 32–33); *The Play of the Secret Diary of Adrian Mole aged 13¾* by Sue Townsend (p 34); from *The Other Side of Truth* by Beverley Naidoo, published by Penguin 2000 , text copyright © Beverley Naidoo, 2000. Reprinted with permission of Penguin Books UK (p 36); 'Like Mother Like, Son' by Pauline Cartledge, *Daily Telegraph*, 3 May 1997. The Telegraph Group. Reprinted with permission (p 37); 'Everyone Sang' by Siegfried Sassoon, from *Collected Poems*. Reprinted with permission of Barbara Levy Literary Agency (p 43); from Winston Churchill's 'Finest Hour 'speech, 18th June 1940. Reprinted with permission of Curtis Brown UK (p 45); from *To Kill a Mockingbird* by Harper Lee, page 14, published by William Heinemann (p 46); from *Animal Farm* by George Orwell. Copyright © 1946 by Sonia Brownell Orwell. Copyright © renewed 1974 by Sonia Orwell. Reprinted by permission of Houghton Mifflin Harcourt Publishing Company, A M Heath for Bill Hamilton as the Literary Executor of the Estate of the late Sonia Brownell Orwell and Penguin Books UK. All rights reserved (p 49); extract from *Holes* by Louis Sachar © Louis Sachar, Holes, Bloomsbury Publishing Plc (p 50); from *Cider With Rosie* by Laurie Lee, reprinted with permission of The Random House Group Limited (p 54); from *My Family and Other Animals* by Gerald Durrell, Puffin (p 55); extracts from 'Not My Best Side' UA Fanthorpe, Peterloo Poets. Reprinted with permission of Dr. R. V. Bailey (pp 60–61); extracts from *World Party: The Rough Guide to the World's Best Festivals*, Penguin. Reprinted with permission of Penguin Books UK (p 66); extracts from *Another Life* by Derek Walcott, published by Jonathan Cape (pp 68–70); Extract from *The Lonely Londoners* by Sam Selvon, published by Penguin page 23. Reprinted by kind permission of the Literary Estate of Sam Selvon (p 75); *A Respectable Trade* by Philippa Gregory. Reprinted by permission of HarperCollins Publishes Ltd © 1996 Philippa Gregory (p 78); Frankenstein by Nick Dear; from *Dreams of Anne Frank* by Bernard Kops, published by Bloomsbury. Reprinted with permission of the publishers (pp 88–89); Leaflet from The Brooke Donkey Charity (p 90); 'The death of handwriting impoverishes us', Melanie McDonagh, *Daily Telegraph*, 26th Feburary 2009, The Telegraph Group. Reprinted with permission (pp 94–95); Bob Stanley article in The Guardian © Guardian News & Media Ltd 2013 (pp 96–97); 'Aunt Julia' by Norman MacCaig, *Collected Poems*, Estate of Norman MacCaig Birlinn Limited (p 98).

Contents

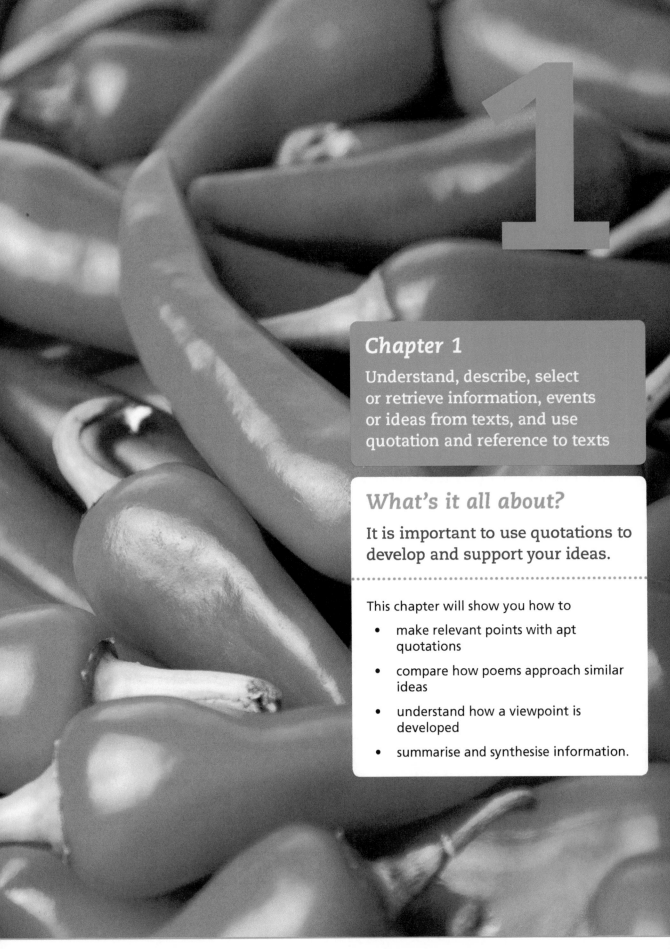

Chapter 1

Understand, describe, select or retrieve information, events or ideas from texts, and use quotation and reference to texts

What's it all about?

It is important to use quotations to develop and support your ideas.

This chapter will show you how to

- make relevant points with apt quotations

- compare how poems approach similar ideas

- understand how a viewpoint is developed

- summarise and synthesise information.

Make relevant points with apt quotations

Learning objective

- select a few words or a word as a quotation to prove your point.

It is important to be able to identify the central ideas in a text, and to select short, apt quotations to prove their points.

Getting you thinking

Below is an extract from Sir Roger Bannister's autobiography. He was the first person to run a mile in under four minutes.

> As we lined up for the start I glanced at the flag again. It fluttered more gently now, and the scene from **Shaw's _Saint Joan_** flashed through my mind, how she, at her desperate moment, waited for the wind to change. Yes, the wind was dropping slightly. This was the moment when I made my decision. The attempt was on.
>
> There was complete silence on the ground... a false start... I felt angry that precious moments during the lull in the wind might be slipping by. The gun fired a second time... Brasher went into the lead and I slipped in effortlessly behind him, feeling tremendously full of running. My legs seemed to meet no resistance at all, as if propelled by some unknown force.
>
> We seemed to be going so slowly! Impatiently I shouted 'Faster!' But Brasher kept his head and did not change the pace.
>
> _The First Four Minutes_ by Roger Bannister

1 In pairs, discuss how the writer makes the race sound exciting. Use short quotations to support your answer.

How does it work?

Read one student's analysis of the text.

> The writer builds up tension by describing the start of the race in minute detail – for example, the flag that 'fluttered more gently now'. In this way, we experience the tense wait for the start through Bannister's eyes as he notices specific things around him, as if time has slowed down.

— point being made

— evidence – a direct quotation

— explanation and analysis of how this effect is created

Glossary

Shaw's _Saint Joan_: a play by George Bernard Shaw about the life and death of St Joan of Arc

2 Write your own paragraph about how Bannister uses punctuation and different sentence lengths in the extract to change the pace or suggest how he is feeling. Comment on exclamation marks and/or **ellipses**. Use a similar format to the example paragraph above.

Glossary

....

ellipses: three dots to indicate a pause or an action that is unfinished

In this extract, Richard Branson explains how he started out in business.

My very first business enterprises, or moneymaking schemes, were not a success, but I learned from them. One Easter holiday, when I was about nine years old and home from prep school, I came up with a great plan. I would grow Christmas trees. Everyone wanted a Christmas tree, so it seemed logical to conclude that quite literally Christmas trees were a cash crop – and what's more, they just grew themselves. Pound signs danced in my eyes. I found out where to get seedlings and sent away for them. As soon as they arrived, I asked my best friend, Nik Powell, to help me plant some 400 seedlings in our field at home. [...] All we had to do was wait for the seedlings to turn into Christmas trees in eighteen months, sell them and count the money. Even at an early age I planned long term.

[...] Sadly, rabbits ate all the seedlings.

Screw It, Let's Do It by Richard Branson

3 How has Richard Branson tried to interest the reader in his first business idea? Use quotations and consider

- what words, phrases and **metaphors** he uses to make his ideas sound exciting

- what details he gives that show the relevance of this event to his later life as a famous, successful businessman.

Glossary

....

metaphors: direct comparisons that describe one thing in terms of another

Check your progress

....

Some progress »

I can select and comment on short, relevant and meaningful quotations.

Good progress »»

I can select short, relevant and meaningful quotations and discuss their meaning in detail.

4 Imagine a celebrity is writing his or her autobiography and has asked you for advice in describing a key moment of his/her life. Use the two extracts to compile five top tips for making the incident sounds interesting to a reader. For example:

> Include plenty of detail, as this makes the situation seem realistic and helps the reader to imagine he/she is there.

Excellent progress »»»

I can use relevant one-word and longer quotations, and analyse their meaning, to securely back up my points.

Compare how poems approach similar ideas

At GCSE level, you will be asked to compare the ways in which two poets create mood and explore or present similar themes in their work.

Getting you thinking

Read this first section of a poem.

Preludes I

The winter evening settles down
With smell of steaks in passageways.
Six o'clock.
The burnt-out ends of smoky days.
And now a gusty shower wraps
The grimy scraps
Of withered leaves about your feet
And newspapers from vacant lots;
The showers beat
On broken blinds and chimney-pots,
And at the corner of the street
A lonely cab-horse steams and stamps.
And then the lighting of the lamps.

T.S. Eliot

1 In pairs, discuss the following questions.

a) What does this poem seem to be about?

b) What is the poem's setting?

c) What mood or atmosphere does the poem create?

Top tip

Take your ideas a stage further by 'zooming in' on particular key words and using them to shape your interpretation

How does it work?

Read what one student has written about the poem.

The poet conveys a sense of deadness through the reference to 'withered leaves'. The adjective 'withered' suggests decay but also an absence of life, an effect also suggested by the 'lighting of the lamps' which is an act done anonymously.

— quotation embedded into sentence

— mention of language features to back up ideas

— more detailed interpretation

Read the opening of this poem.

Friday Night at the Royal Station Hotel

Light spreads darkly downwards from the high
Clusters of lights over empty chairs
That face each other, coloured differently.
Through open doors, the dining-room declares
A larger loneliness of knives and glass
And silence laid like carpet. A porter reads
An unsold evening paper. Hours pass,
And all the salesmen have gone back to Leeds,
Leaving full ashtrays in the Conference Room.

In shoeless corridors, the lights burn. How
Isolated, like a fort, it is –
The headed paper, made for writing home
(If home existed) letters of exile: *Now*
Night comes on. Waves fold behind villages.

Philip Larkin

2 In pairs, find three pieces of evidence that suggest absence or loneliness in the poem (for example, the word 'loneliness' itself, an image, a detail, a weary rhythm or tone).

3 Now compare how the two poems deal with the themes of absence and loneliness. You could start with a general comment, followed by specific details.

4 Write a further sentence or two about loneliness or absence of life in each of the poems. Begin with a general statement, and then add a specific point or two for each poem.

Apply your skills

5 Write up a full comparison of the poems in five paragraphs. Make sure you use at least one quotation to back up each point, and explain its effect on the reader.

Top tip

Remember that you can move from the broad similarities between two writers' approaches to the finer differences.

Check your progress

Some progress 》

I can read across both poems and pick out the most relevant points.

Good progress 》》

I can compare specific ideas in the poems, referring to relevant quotations.

Excellent progress 》》》

I can explore the impressions that different poems make on a reader, comparing them with apt quotations.

Understand how a viewpoint is developed

Learning objective

- understand how a particular viewpoint is developed.

You should be able to trace a viewpoint in a text, and support your ideas about it by using precise quotations and examining their impact on the reader.

Getting you thinking

In pairs, read this headline and sub-heading of a newspaper article.

First the snow, now the ice

Britain in the grip of harshest winter weather for 18 years

David Brown, *The Times*, 2009

1 From the headline and sub-heading, what do you think the main focus of the article will be? What feelings are the headings meant to **evoke**?

Glossary

evoke: to bring to mind or conjure up

superlative: an adjective that signals the strongest or highest level of something. Although superlatives often end in 'est' ('bravest', 'coldest'), you may need to use 'most' for the same effect with other words ('most terrible' not 'terriblest').

How does it work?

The viewpoint of a text is the opinion or attitude that the writer expresses towards an issue, idea or person. Such viewpoints can often be traced through a text from start to finish.

In the article, the headline and sub-heading set the tone for what follows. For example, note the use of a powerful noun ('grip') and a **superlative** in the heading ('harshest'). The viewpoint expressed is 'we should be worried about this!'

Now you try it

Below is the opening of another newspaper article from the same day.

Snowbound Britain

Road, rail and airport bosses face anger as services grind to a halt

Large swathes of Britain came to a standstill yesterday in the grip of the worst snowstorms for 18 years. Despite five days of severe weather warnings, transport bosses still appeared to have been completely caught out as up to a foot of snow fell across the country, bringing rail, air and road networks to a halt.

They faced a growing public backlash as one in five workers was left stranded at home, at an estimated cost to the economy of £1.2 billion.

In London, all bus services were cancelled for the first time in living memory, as a network which had carried on running during the Blitz – and during much worse conditions in 1963 – proved unable to deal with six inches of snow. Cancelled Tube trains added to the chaos in the city.

[...] As hundreds of train services and flights were stopped and drivers faced treacherous conditions on ungritted roads, angry commuters demanded to know why the severe weather warnings had not been properly heeded.

Nigel Humphries, of the Association of British Drivers, said there could be no excuse for the failure of transport authorities to prepare for 'entirely predictable weather conditions'.

Gordon Raynor, *Daily Telegraph*, 2009

2 Read the newspaper article carefully and decide what the viewpoint is. Who do you think the writer blames for the transport problems?

3 What individual word choices best convey the writer's viewpoint? Continue the table below.

Short quotation from the text	Why have these particular words been used?	What does this tell us about the writer's attitude?
'services grind to a halt'	'grind' brings to mind the unpleasant breakdown of an engine	suggests an unplanned and inefficient breakdown

4 Choose two quotations and write a paragraph on each, explaining the writer's viewpoint and the effect of the words or phrases he has chosen.

> **Top tip**
>
> Use short quotations in your answers, and try to discuss the effect of individual words.

Apply your skills

5 Now write an article from the viewpoint of the transport authorities, in which they put forward a case for their defence. Use words and phrases that vividly convey their viewpoint, such as

- expressions of how unusual the weather is ('freak weather')

- superlatives to express the power of the weather ('heaviest snowfall')

- descriptions of how hard they worked ('bravely facing the terrible conditions').

Check your progress

Some progress
I can use my own opinion and at least one quotation to support my ideas about viewpoint in a text.

Good progress
I can trace a viewpoint through a text and support my ideas with information.

Excellent progress
I can explain how a viewpoint has been developed.

Summarise and synthesise information

When you are reading longer texts, you may need to reduce the text to its most important parts so the information can be used for other purposes.

Getting you thinking

Imagine you are researching a holiday in Marrakech. Read the travel brochure below.

Marrakech Holiday – A Week in the Red City

Detailed Itinerary

Day 1 – Arrival in Marrakech
Your time in Marrakech today will be determined by the arrival time of your flight at the spacious new terminal building at Marrakech Menara Airport. You will be met by our local representative and transferred by private vehicle to your accommodation.

Day 2 – Exploring the Souks and Djemaa el Fna
For first-time visitors to the medina of Marrakech, a great way of getting to grips with this magical city is on a guided orientation walk. The famous souks of Marrakech offer an intoxicating passage to Africa's most famous meeting place – the huge medieval square of Djemaa el Fna. Here, at the heart of the old city, acrobats and jugglers, snake charmers, beggars, boxers, musicians, and fresh juice and food sellers all compete for your attention – and a few **dirhams** in the process. It is easy to spend several hours wandering the square, sipping mint tea and savouring the utter assault on your senses. As night falls, take a seat in one of the restaurants that overlook the square and watch the scene unfold. With the conflicting sounds from musicians and singers, and thousands of tiny white lights illuminating the swirling smoke rising from food stalls, expect a night you'll never forget!

www.specialistmorocco.com

Glossary

souks: markets in Arabic cities

dirhams: Moroccan currency

1 What important travel information from Day 1 do you need to make a note of?

2 What information in the itinerary is *not* vital to know?

How does it work?

When noting key information, you need to decide what is important to your needs and what is not. For example:

> spacious new terminal building at Marrakech Menara Airport.

adjectives promote the qualities of the terminal

proper noun tells you the airport's name

It is vital to know the name of the airport; it is less vital to know what the terminal is like.

Summarising key aspects from a text often means **paraphrasing**. For example:

> Day 1: Arrive at Marrakech Menara airport, meet rep, <u>travel to lodgings</u>.

The phrase 'travel to lodgings' replaces and shortens the phrase 'transferred by private vehicle to your accommodation'.

Glossary

paraphrasing: putting information into your own words

Now you try it

If you were looking for reasons to visit Marrakech you might notice words such as 'magical', 'intoxicating', 'famous souks', 'huge medieval square' and 'old city'.

 3 Which of the following three summaries best **synthesises** these attractions?

- Marrakech is really magical because it has so many famous and large buildings and squares.

- Marrakech is a charismatic, ancient place with memorable architecture.

- Marrakech is well known all over the world.

Glossary

synthesises: brings together different elements in a concise way

Check your progress

Some progress »
I can select relevant information from a text.

Good progress »»
I can identify and summarise relevant information from a text and put it in my own words.

Excellent progress »»»
I can synthesise different elements from a text in my own words.

Apply your skills

 4 Now write your own short summary in response to this question:

> Why should a tourist in Marrakech visit the 'heart of the city'?

Make sure you paraphrase the extract's descriptions of what can be seen and experienced. Try to synthesise your ideas into concise sentences.

Check your progress

Some progress

- [ ] I can read across several texts and pick out the most relevant points.
- [ ] I can select and comment on short, relevant and meaningful quotations.
- [ ] I can make accurate points about viewpoint in a text and support them with my own opinion and a quotation.
- [ ] I can select relevant parts of information in a text.

Good progress

- [ ] I can pick out appropriate evidence from across a range of texts.
- [ ] I can select short, apt quotations and discuss their meaning in detail.
- [ ] I can trace the development of a viewpoint.
- [ ] I can identify relevant information from a text and put it in my own words.

Excellent progress

- [ ] I can analyse the effectiveness of different quotations.
- [ ] I can use apt one-word quotations and analyse their meaning.
- [ ] I can explain how a viewpoint has been developed.
- [ ] I can summarise and synthesise different elements from a text in my own words.

2

Chapter 2
Deduce, infer or interpret information, events or ideas from texts

What's it all about?

It is important for you to explore texts more deeply in order to interpret their meanings.

This chapter will show you how to

- make inferences from challenging texts

- develop interpretations across texts

- consider the wider implications of themes, events and ideas in texts

- explore the connotations of words and images

- explore what can be inferred from the finer details of texts.

Make inferences from challenging texts

Learning objective
- understand the implied meanings of poems.

To make inferences from what you read means that you look beyond the obvious meaning. For example, look at this **couplet** from 'Refugee Blues' by W. H. Auden – written about Hitler's Germany.

> Walked through a wood, saw the birds in the trees;
> They had no politicians and sang at their ease

It **implies** that politicians stop people living freely, but never actually states this. The reader or listener **infers** the meaning.

Glossary

couplet: a pair of rhyming lines

implies: hints at but doesn't say directly

infers: works out for him or herself

Getting you thinking

Read this extract from a poem. It states some things but implies others.

Early Bird Blues

I am the early bird.
I have worn out my shoes
Simply because I heard
First come was first to choose.
One of my talents is avoiding queues.

I never ask how long
I shall be made to wait.
I have done nothing wrong.
I don't exaggerate.
To state the obvious, I'm never late.

Why has the queue not grown?
Nobody hears me speak.
I stand here all alone
Which makes me look unique
But even so, the worm avoids my beak.

Sophie Hannah

1. Explain how this poem takes a fresh look at the **proverb** 'the early bird catches the worm'.

2. Do we ever find out what the narrator is waiting for? What effect does this have?

3. What lines suggest – or *imply* – sadness?

Glossary

proverb: a well-known saying that states a supposed truth or a piece of advice

4 Look at the title of the poem. What do you know about the 'blues', and what can you infer about the poem from this term?

How does it work?

Nothing is explicitly stated in the poem but we can infer various relevant meanings. The proverb 'the early bird catches the worm' usually suggests that promptness or hard work leads to success, but the speaker here is first in a queue of one. No one else even wants what she rushes for, and she does not get her reward.

Blues music, to which the poem's title also refers, is generally sad but can include a wry smile about human suffering – just like the poem itself.

Now you try it

5 What can you *infer* about the narrator in the poem? She states she is a bird. Is she?

6 Explain how and why the poet adopts a **persona** (a bird).

7 What can you infer about this persona from the type of phrases the poet uses?

Apply your skills

Blues songs often use personas. A famous example is 'The Little Red Rooster' written by Willie Dixon, where we *infer* that the song about a farmyard cockerel 'too lazy to crow the day' is really about the singer's unhappy love life.

8 Think about writing your own persona poem. What kind of bird would you use to imply the following:

a) joy   c) despair

b) loneliness   d) boredom?

Explain your reasons for choosing each type of bird.

9 Now have a go at writing your own persona poem. Use the same form as 'Early Bird Blues' if it helps. Perhaps make your sentences fit the persona – for example, an owl might use lots of complex sentences and see things in a piercingly clear way.

Remember to *imply* your situation and feelings through the persona rather than stating them openly.

Glossary

persona: a role or character that a writer adopts in a text

Check your progress

Some progress

I can recognise implied meanings.

Good progress

I can infer meanings and explain how they work.

Excellent progress

I can identify and explain different levels of meaning in texts.

Develop interpretations across texts

It is often necessary to interpret information from different parts of a text. For example, in a newspaper article you might learn the age of a fever victim at the beginning – then later that they are the youngest-ever victim of that fever, which makes the fact more shocking. You might find out something that changes your whole view of the text.

Getting you thinking

Read this opening stanza of a poem called 'Symptoms'.

Symptoms

Although you have given me a stomach upset,
Weak knees, a lurching heart, a fuzzy brain,
A high-pitched laugh, a monumental phone bill,
A feeling of unworthiness, sharp pain
When you are somewhere else, a guilty conscience,
A longing, and a dread of what's in store,
A pulse rate for the Guinness Book of Records –
Life now is better than it was before.

Sophie Hannah

1 What does the final line – when taken with the rest of the stanza – suggest about being in love?

How does it work?

Here is a model answer to the question above.

> The stanza lists lots of negatives about being in love – 'stomach upset...a dread of what's in store' – but the final line, 'Life now is better than it was before', turns the whole poem around. The final line suggests, in relation to the rest of the stanza, that although there can be many difficult experiences when you are in love, life is better for it. It implies that all the negatives are worth it. The start of the poem sets up this conclusion by beginning 'Although...'

The student has thought about the different information given in the final line of the poem and has related it back to the rest of the stanza.

2 In pairs, mark up a director's copy of this extract from *Romeo and Juliet*. Write in the margins what you want the actors to do – what gestures, expressions or actions they should perform as they speak – at each stage of the script.

ROMEO   If I profane with my unworthiest hand
          This holy shrine, the gentle sin is this.
          My lips, two blushing pilgrims, ready stand
          To smooth that rough touch with a tender kiss.
JULIET   Good pilgrim, you do wrong your hand
            too much,
          Which **mannerly devotion** shows in this.
          For saints have hands that pilgrims' hands
            do touch,
          And palm to palm is **holy palmers**' kiss.
ROMEO   Have not saints lips, and holy palmers, too?
JULIET   Ay, pilgrim, lips that they must use in prayer.
ROMEO   O, then, dear saint, let lips do what hands do.
          They pray, grant thou, lest faith turn to despair.
JULIET   Saints do not move, though grant for
            prayers' sake.
ROMEO   Then move not, while my prayer's effect I take.
(They kiss.)

3 Life for Romeo and Juliet certainly seems better at the end of this extract than it did in the first line! Find evidence from the text to back this up.

4 Copy out the last word of each line. What rhyme pattern is made? Does it change at the end? If so, what effect does it create at the moment before they kiss? (Try speaking the final couplet aloud with your partner.)

5 What **figurative language** does Shakespeare use to create his effects?

Apply your skills

6 Write up answers to the following questions.

a) Does Romeo and Juliet's relationship change in these 14 lines?

b) What is suggested by Romeo referring to hands in line 1 but a kiss by line 4? What has happened to Juliet's resistance (in line 10) by the end of line 14?

Glossary
....

mannerly devotion: behaviour suitable to a holy place

holy palmers: Christian pilgrims (holding a palm leaf to show they've been to the Holy Land)

figurative language: language that isn't literal in meaning – for example, the religious metaphor here of 'blushing pilgrims' for Romeo's lips

Check your progress
....

Some progress »
I can annotate a text to show my understanding of different stages of a text.

Good progress »
I can analyse examples from different stages of a text that focus on a particular theme.

Excellent progress »»
I can produce an in-depth response to a text based on my ideas about each stage of its development.

Consider the wider implications of themes, events and ideas in texts

Learning objective

• understand how and why a writer might choose to write about a theme.

When you read, you make deductions about what is happening – these deductions are often to do with ideas, **themes**, characters or events. You also need to think about why the writer chooses to write about these ideas or themes in the way he or she does.

> **Glossary**
>
> **themes:** ideas that runs throughout a text

Getting you thinking

In pairs, read this description of a boy in modern London.

> I didn't come to London straight away. I may be homeless and unemployed but I'm not stupid. I'd read about London. I knew the streets down here weren't paved with gold. I knew there were hundreds of people – thousands, in fact – sleeping rough and begging for **coppers**. But that's just the point, see? In Bradford I stuck out like a sore thumb because there weren't many of us. The police down here have got used to seeing kids kipping in doorways, and mostly they leave you alone. In Bradford I was getting moved on every hour or so. I was getting no sleep at all, and practically no money. People up there haven't got used to beggars yet. They're embarrassed. They'll make large detours to avoid passing close to you, and if somebody does come within earshot and you ask for change, they look startled and hurry on by.
>
> *Stone Cold* by Robert Swindells

> **Glossary**
>
> **coppers:** small coins

1 What do we find out about homelessness in

a) Bradford

b) London?

2 What can you deduce about the narrator's *character*? Write a paragraph giving at least three examples.

How does it work?

The writer is obviously concerned about homelessness and creates a character to represent and comment on the issue. The reader can deduce from the character some key details about the plight of the homeless.

Now you try it

Read this second extract from the same book.

> I strode out of the station with my backpack and bed-roll, and it felt like a new beginning. This was London, wasn't it? The centre, where it all happens. It's big, it's fast, and it's full of opportunities. Nobody knows you. Where you're from and what's gone before – that's your business. It's a clean sheet – you can invent your own past and call yourself anything you choose.

3 In pairs, answer the questions below.

a) What positive ideas about London does the text suggest?

b) What negative ideas about London were suggested in the first extract?

c) What does the boy's move from Bradford to London mean for him?

d) What can you deduce about why he is glad to leave Bradford behind?

4 Now try to do these activities by yourself.

a) Find an example of an active or positive verb/mood in this extract to contrast with passive or negative ones in the previous extract.

b) Find a similar contrast of past and present tense in the two extracts.

c) Explain how this difference in grammar reflects the negative and positive moods of the two extracts.

Check your progress

Some progress

I can understand how characters and themes develop in a novel.

Good progress

I can answer questions about, and provide evidence for, themes in the texts I read.

Excellent progress

I can make inferences about what I think will happen in a text, and give reasons for them.

Apply your skills

5 Think about the two extracts you have read.

a) Overall, how does the writer make you feel about children sleeping on the streets and begging?

b) Why do you think he chose to write in the first person about being homeless?

6 Both extracts are taken from a novel – *Stone Cold* by Robert Swindells. What do you think the book is about? What do you think the main themes of the book are? Explain your answers in detail, using evidence from the extracts.

Explore the connotations of words and images

When you read, you need to consider not only what words and images *show* (their **denotation**), but also what they *suggest* (their **connotation**). For example, the word 'red' can be used literally to describe the colour, but it can also *connote* passion, anger or romance.

Glossary

denotation: the literal meaning of a word

connotation: what a word suggests or implies

Getting you thinking

Read this description of a scene in a girls' school.

The January term started with a scene of sheer disaster. A muddy excavator was chewing its way across the netball-court, breakfasting on the tarmac with **sinuous** lunges and terrifying swings of its yellow dinosaur neck. One of the stone balls had been knocked off the gate-posts, and lay in crushed fragments, like a Malteser trodden on by a giant. The entrance to the science wing was blocked with a pile of **ochreous** clay, and curved glazed drainpipes were heaped like school dinners' macaroni.

The girls hung round in groups. One girl came back from the indoor toilets saying Miss Bowker was phoning the Council, and using words that Eliza Bottom had nearly been expelled for last term...

The next girl came back from the toilet saying Miss Bowker was nearly crying.

Which was definitely a lie, because here was Miss Bowker now, come out to address them in her best sheepskin coat. Though she was wearing fresh make-up, and her eyes were suspiciously bright, her famous chin was up. She was brief, and to the point. There was an underground leak in the central heating; till it was mended, they would be using the old Harvest Road boys' school. They would march across now, by forms, in good order, in charge of the prefects.

'The Boys' Toilets' by Robert Westall, from *Ghost Stories*

1 In groups, discuss what kind of atmosphere is built up in this passage.

2 Pick three images from the passage that help to build up this atmosphere. On one side of a sheet of A3 paper, draw what you think each image literally describes (its *denotation*), and on the other draw what it suggests (its *connotations*). For example, 'breakfasting' *denotes* the act of eating but *connotes* a monster (a digger) eating a school.

Glossary

sinuous: supple or bending

ochreous: yellow or brown in colour

How does it work?

Familiar and domestic things, such as macaroni and Maltesers, are made grotesque here. 'Sinuous' is horribly snake-like, and the excavator's 'dinosaur neck' and 'chewing' action make it sound like a dangerous animal. The atmosphere is both funny and frightening – even the famously chin-up Miss Bowker feels fragile!

Now you try it

In this next extract, the girls are on their way to the boys' school.

> Then the marching columns came to a miserable little hump-backed bridge over a solitary railway-line, empty and rusting. Beyond were the same kind of houses; but afflicted by some dreadful disease, of which the symptoms were a rash of small window-panes, flaking paint, overgrown funereal privet-hedges and sagging gates that would never shut again. And then it seemed to grow colder still, as the slum-clearances started, a great empty plain of broken brick, and the wind hit them full, sandpapering faces and sending grey berets cartwheeling into the wilderness.

Think about how imagery is used here – in particular, through **personification** – to create a strong mood or atmosphere.

3 What mood is created by the following images?

a) 'a miserable little hump-backed bridge'

b) 'a solitary railway-line'

c) 'houses…afflicted by some dreadful disease'

4 How does the description of the weather add to the mood?

5 What does the word 'funereal' suggest about the privet hedges?

Apply your skills

6 What atmosphere and expectations have been set up in these extracts? Write up your analysis, including the information and ideas that you gave in your earlier responses. Analyse how the connotations of the words and images that have been chosen help to establish a mood.

Glossary

personification: giving a non-human object or thing human characteristics

Check your progress

Some progress

I can work out how images create a mood or atmosphere.

Good progress

I can analyse the denotations and connotations of words and images.

Excellent progress

I can analyse language, including the connotations of words and images, and link it to the overall purpose and effect of a text.

Explore what can be inferred from the finer details of texts

It is important that you make *inferences* about what you read. It is also important to *comment in detail* on these inferences, explaining your deductions and interpretations with close reference to the text.

Getting you thinking

Read this extract from the beginning of a novel.

'Robin won't give you any trouble,' said Auntie Lynn. 'He's very quiet.'

Anthea knew how quiet Robin was. At present he was sitting under the table and, until Auntie Lynn mentioned his name, she had forgotten that he was there. Auntie Lynn put a carrier bag on the armchair.

'There's plenty of clothes, so you won't need to do any washing, and there's a spare pair of pyjamas in case – well, you know. In case...'

'Yes,' said Mum firmly [...].

Mum almost told Auntie Lynn to stop worrying and have a good time, which would have been a mistake because Auntie Lynn was going up North to a funeral.

Auntie Lynn was not really an Aunt, but she had once been at school with Anthea's mum [...] Robin was not anything much, except four years old, and he looked a lot younger; probably because nothing ever happened to him. Auntie Lynn kept no pets that might give Robin germs, and never bought him toys that had sharp corners to dent him or wheels that could be swallowed. He wore balaclava helmets and bobble hats in winter to protect his tender ears, and a knitted vest under his shirt in summer in case he overheated himself and caught a chill from his own sweat.

Nothing to be Afraid of by Jan Mark

 1 What kind of things can you infer about 'Auntie' Lynn's treatment of her son? Work through the extract, supporting your comments and inferences with quotations and explanations.

How does it work?

You might infer that Auntie Lynn is quite overprotective towards her son. For example, Anthea's mother had to tell her to 'stop worrying', suggesting that she may not normally leave Robin with other people. From 'just in case', you might infer that Auntie Lynn means Robin might wet the bed, but doesn't want to say this aloud.

Now you try it

 2 Read the extract again. This time, write a detailed response explaining what you infer about the *character* of Robin.

Apply your skills

Read the next extract from the story.

> His face was as pale and flat as a saucer of milk, and his eyes floated in it like drops of cod-liver oil. This was not so surprising, as he was full to the back teeth with cod-liver oil; also with extract of malt, concentrated orange juice and calves-foot jelly. When you picked him up you expected him to squelch, like a hot-water bottle full of half-set custard.
>
> Anthea lifted the tablecloth and looked at him.
> 'Hello, Robin.'
> Robin stared at her with his flat eyes and went back to sucking his woolly doggy that had flat eyes also, of sewn-on felt, because glass ones might find their way into Robin's appendix and cause damage.

3 Discuss in pairs what is implied about Robin in this second extract.

4 Look back at your response to Activity 2. Adapt and develop it, using the ideas that arose in your discussion in Activity 3, so that it covers both extracts.

Check your progress

Some progress
I can make inferences about a character's behaviour.

Good progress
I can write a detailed response about a character, based on the inferences I have made.

Excellent progress
I can infer meaning from a text and use these points to develop an in-depth discussion, which I can record in a detailed piece of writing.

Check your progress

Some progress

- [ ] I can understand the purpose of different types of words.
- [ ] I can annotate a text to show my understanding of ideas.
- [ ] I can understand the wider implications of a text.
- [ ] I can understand how a text can affect readers.
- [ ] I can make inferences about different parts of a novel.

Good progress

- [ ] I can make inferences based on different parts of poems.
- [ ] I can understand that extracts from different texts can be linked to a theme.
- [ ] I can understand and explain the wider implications of a text.
- [ ] I can understand questions and give detailed answers.
- [ ] I can understand literary terms, such as denotation and connotation.

Excellent progress

- [ ] I can compare ideas in detail with explanations.
- [ ] I can develop an in-depth response based on my inferences.
- [ ] I can understand and analyse the wider implications of a text.
- [ ] I can understand the purpose of language and use analysis to back up my ideas.
- [ ] I can discuss my ideas and apply what I have learned to a detailed piece of writing.

3

Chapter 3

Identify and comment on the structure and organisation of texts

What's it all about?

You need to be aware of how writers structure text to shape meaning and develop ideas.

This chapter will show you how to

- comment on how successfully writers have opened their stories

- explore how writers structure a whole text

- recognise and discuss the effects of a range of structural features in a text

- comment on writers' use of narrative structure to shape meaning

- compare the organisation and development of a theme through a whole text.

Comment on how successfully writers have opened their stories

Recognising whether a writer has opened a story well – and knowing what makes one story opening better than another – will help you to discuss texts with confidence.

Getting you thinking

Read these two story openings.

> **A**
>
> Prince Latarno slowly rose to his feet, casting one malignant glance at the prisoner before him.
>
> 'You have heard', he said, 'what is alleged against you. Have you anything to say in your defence?'

> **B**
>
> Only kids believed City Cemetery was haunted. But that changed the Halloween night fourteen-year-old Willard Armbruster disappeared. His body was never found.

1 Identify the different ways these two stories begin. Do the writers introduce any of the following features?

- plot
- dialogue
- setting
- narration
- character
- conflict
- genre

2 How successful do you think these openings are?

How does it work?

Both writers hook their readers with their openings. The first writer makes clever use of *character*, *dialogue* and *conflict*. The second employs *setting*, *genre* and the beginnings of *plot*. Each opening makes us want to find out more.

Writers might use techniques such as *first-* or *second-person narration*, *short* and *long sentences*, or *times* and *dates* to grab the reader's interest. A short sentence such as 'His body was never found' intrigues readers and encourages them to read on to find out what happened to Willard Armbruster. Long sentences can heighten tension by keeping readers waiting to see what might happen next.

C

'How long has your husband been missing?' Detective Whittier asked.

Mrs Brenner had dark angry eyes. 'Since this morning at ten o'clock.'

D

The hunter found a human head propped up by the roots of the tree. It was an old head, little more than a skull, with grinning jaws and gaping eye sockets.

'I wonder how that got here,' he muttered half to himself.

E

It was an eighty-cow dairy, and the troop of milkers, regular and supernumerary, were all at work; for, though the time of the year was as yet but early April, the feed lay entirely in water-meadows, and the cows were 'in full pail'.

F

The overcast sky causes him to snap on the Firebird's headlights. Even before reaching the on-ramp he is travelling at 60 mph. Shoved between his legs is a cold can of Budweiser that stains the crotch of his tight tan slacks.

 3 Imagine that you are a book editor. You have been given these story openings to assess. Which is the best?

Give each opening a mark out of five. Explain why you have awarded this mark, using the points below to guide you.

Think about

- how characters and settings have been introduced
- whether a conflict is established
- whether the readers are left with unanswered questions
- how dialogue is used
- whether the extract makes you want to read on.

Check your progress

Some progress

I can comment on how different narrative viewpoints affect the way in which a story opening is written and structured.

Good progress

I can discuss the way in which narrative viewpoint affects how a story opening is written and structured.

Apply your skills

 4 Look at openings C and D with a partner. Discuss how each story's narrative viewpoint is likely to affect the way the story opening is written and structured. What difference might it make if opening C was told from Detective Whittier's or Mrs Brenner's point of view?

Excellent progress

I can analyse in detail the way in which narrative viewpoint affects how a story opening is written and structured, and the reasons for this.

Explore how writers structure a whole text

Learning objective

• discuss the structure of a whole text in detail.

Being able to analyse an article and recognise the techniques that writers use to create an effective structure will help you to discuss texts in detail.

Getting you thinking

Read this section of an article from the *Mail Online*:

No relatives. No turkey. A £30 Ikea tree. My perfect Xmas!

Christmas is a magical occasion, a time to reconnect with loved ones and honour tradition.

In the case of my family, that means ritual humiliation, the solemn resurrection of old feuds, a festive explosion of colourful language — and, if things really go with a bang, maybe even a trip to A&E.

And this is the week it all kicks off. In Arndale centres across the land, perma-tanned D-list celebs shiver in the late November air, switching on lights in a frenzy of manufactured jollity.

Bing Crosby warbles from every shop door, soppy TV ads fight for our attention and catalogues collect on the doormat like snowdrifts. Only 35 panic-buying days left, folks.

Meanwhile, the so-called festive fun is just days away. In Hyde Park and other licensed locations, the final touches are being put to the annual 'treat' that is Winter Wonderland.

Here, families can share the joy of paying over the odds for a nasty slice of greasy Bavarian sausage and queue for several hours to have their little ones sit on the red polyester-clad knee of a disgruntled seasonal worker. Entry may be free, but it will cost you at least £100 in rip-off rides to get out alive.

Welcome to Christmas in modern Britain. Not so much a celebration of the birth of Christ as an annual exercise in collective mania.

Sarah Vine, *Mail Online*, 20 November 2013

1 What is the theme of this article?

2 How is this theme developed in each of the main paragraphs and returned to in the conclusion?

3 How does the writer engage the reader's interest?

How does it work?

Writers for newspapers and online blogs usually set the agenda for an article right at the start. They often use a title or headline that indicates the theme, include a topic sentence in the opening paragraph to explain the focus of the article, and then reiterate the theme throughout. Articles like the one on page 30, which aren't about serious news, often use a conversational tone to engage the reader's interest.

Now you try it

 4 Make notes about how the writer uses the following features or techniques to develop her theme.

a) topic sentences to introduce and reiterate main themes/ideas

b) references to time and place to shape the article

c) connectives to link paragraphs and sentences

d) references to everyday images that readers will recognise and associate with Christmas.

Apply your skills

 5 What do *you* think about Christmas (or another seasonal holiday)? Write an article that is based on your own thoughts and experiences. Choose a tone – will you make it serious or witty? Imagine your article will be posted online, and think about the extra features you could use on the webpage to add interest.

Check your progress

Some progress

I can comment on how different narrative viewpoints affect the way in which a story opening is written and structured.

Good progress

I can discuss the way in which narrative viewpoint affects how a story opening is written and structured.

Excellent progress

I can analyse in detail the way in which narrative viewpoint affects how a story opening is written and structured, and the reasons for this.

Recognise and discuss the effects of a range of structural features in a text

Learning objective

- spot and discuss features that writers use to help them structure texts.

Recognising structural features will help you to discuss texts and their features in detail, exploring their effects.

Getting you thinking

Read this opening of the stage play *Dreams of Anne Frank*.

Scene 1

Darkness. A man enters. His clothes are formal. He is well dressed, spick and span, almost out of keeping with the scene he has entered. This is **Otto Frank**. *He lifts the diary from on top of the pile of clothes and speaks quietly without undue emotion.*

OTTO   I'm Otto Frank. Anne Frank was my daughter, and she was very special. I survived the war. Somehow. Anne didn't. Survival was random. Pure chance. That morning when our liberators arrived, I just sat there. Numb. The gates were open but I had no spirit to get up and run. I knew then that my wife was dead, and my neighbours. And my children were God knows where. I was breathing, yet I was dead. We were all dead, those departed and those still there on that morning. The gates were open and everything was incredibly silent and peaceful. All the guards had disappeared, as if they had been spirited away in the night, and that morning for the first time in ages I heard a bird singing. I think it was a blackbird because its song was so beautiful. It couldn't have been a nightingale. They avoided the skies above Auschwitz. Then we heard the sound of guns and great armored vehicles on the move. Getting closer. Russian soldiers appeared. With chocolate cigarettes, **liniment** and bandages. We didn't cheer. We just sat there slumped and staring. Nobody spoke. The sun was so bright and the heat so soaked into my bones. And then one soldier started to play his accordion. Suddenly someone danced. In slow motion.

Glossary

liniment: a cream to relieve pain

Others joined in. More and more. Dancing. Dancing. Soon, everyone who could stand on two legs was dancing. And laughing. And crying. I watched. I just watched. I loved my daughters. Margot and Anne. That goes without saying. But Anne was special. She didn't survive the war. But her words, her story, her secrets, her dreams are all here in this book. The diary of Anne Frank. (*He opens the diary.*)

(*The lights cross-fade, merging into the next scene.*)

Scene 2
Anne appears, holding up a yellow star.

Dreams of Anne Frank by Bernard Kops

1 How does the playwright use stage directions (the words in italic) to set the scene?

2 What does this opening tell you about the type of play this will be and about the main characters?

3 What structural features does the playwright use to make the opening dramatic and lead into the rest of the play?

How does it work?

Playwrights use a range of structural conventions to set the scene and introduce the characters in their plays. These can include

- stage directions (such as music, sound effects and instructions for where characters should be on stage)

- narration (usually by the central character)

- juxtaposition and framed action (such as when Otto Frank opens Anne's diary here and also 'opens' the flashback in time).

Now you try it

Now read the opening of this stage play.

Music: The Mole Overture.

At the end of the Overture, **Adrian** *comes to the front of the stage. He talks directly to the audience.*

ADRIAN   This is just my luck! I've come all the way from Leicester to hear a lecture about **George Eliot** only to be thwarted at the last minute because the American lecturer missed Concorde. What am I going to do now? I'm doing George Eliot for my English Literature project. I've written him loads of letters, but he hasn't replied to one. Still, with a bit of luck I might be able to mingle with a few intellectuals in the foyer.

He looks round at the audience.

There's loads here tonight. But I bet *they* don't live an ordinary life like me. No, they're lucky, they go home to book-lined studies and intellectual families. Perhaps when my diary is discovered people will understand the torment of being a thirteen and three-quarter-year-old intellectual. Until then I'll just have to put up with the charade that is my family life. I bet **Malcolm Muggeridge**'s family didn't carry on like mine did on New Year's Eve.

The lights go up to show the New Year's Eve party. Grandma and **Mrs Lucas** *are sitting on the sofa.* **Pauline** *and* **Mr Lucas** *are dancing together.* **George** *is drinking from a can of lager.* **Adrian** *joins* **Nigel** *at centre stage. Everyone, including* **Adrian**, *is wearing a party hat.*

The Play of The Secret Diary of Adrian Mole, aged 13¾ by Sue Townsend

Glossary

George Eliot: a Victorian writer whose real name was Mary Ann Evans

Malcolm Muggeridge: a journalist and writer who later became a moral and religious campaigner

4   In pairs, talk about how the playwright uses the stage directions to include visual and sound effects that establish the mood and tone of the play.

5 What structural features does the playwright use to give us a sense of character and situation? Make notes on

- what Adrian's words and narration reveal about his character
- the effect of juxtaposing his references to George Eliot, Concorde and intellectual life with the characters, props and actions of the New Year's Eve party
- the use of lighting and flashbacks in the extract.

Apply your skills

6 What similarities and differences are there in the ways these two plays open? Note down your ideas about

- the mood of each play
- what the audience sees and hears
- the use of juxtaposition and its effect
- the use of flashbacks and its effect
- the use of a narrator and its effect
- **symbolism** in each play.

7 Now write up your answer, using evidence from both extracts.

You could start:

> Both playwrights create a sense of mood before either character speaks. Bernard Kops does this through his use of darkness, while Sue Townsend does this through her use of music. We gain an impression of solemnity and sadness in Kops's play through this and Otto's formal clothing. It contrasts with the ridiculousness of Adrian Mole's intellectual pretensions and reluctant presence at the New Year's Eve party.

8 What about Anne's life suggests tragedy and what in Adrian's requires comedy? Do you think some comedy can also be tragic?

Glossary

symbolism: where an object is used to represent something else

Check your progress

Some progress
I can recognise the way in which a playscript is organised and structured.

Good progress
I can recognise and discuss the way in which a playscript is organised, and comment on the effects of structural features.

Excellent progress
I can compare how two playscripts are organised and structured, and explain the effects of structural features.

Comment on writers' use of narrative structure to shape meaning

Learning objective

- discuss the ways in which writers structure texts to help create drama, suggest character, indicate a backstory and develop plot.

One of the most important ways in which a writer organises a text is how he or she places it in time – for example, through the choice of tense or tenses.

Getting you thinking

Read this extract taken from the novel *The Other Side of Truth*. In it, Sade and her brother Femi have arrived in London illegally from Nigeria. They are being questioned by police over an incident in a video shop.

'Do we know if they speak English?' asked Cool Gaze.
'Oh, they speak English all right. I heard 'em!' declared Video Man.
Cool Gaze now towered over them.
'Look. If you've done nothing wrong, there's no need to be frightened.'

Papa has read the piece of paper and Joseph opens the gate. Men in khaki uniform and black berets surge into the yard. Papa is surrounded. Mama lets out a small cry.
'Stay here!' she orders the children and rushes out of the sitting room to get to the yard. By the time she sprints down the steps, the police have hustled Papa out of the gates.
'Where are you taking him?' Mama cries.

Sade glimpses Papa's white shirt among the khaki as police push him into the back of their truck. No one answers Mama. The children run outside. When they reach Mama, the truck is already roaring down the road.

Sade had never felt so cold in all her life. Frozen inside and out. None of the people standing in front of her and Femi made any sense.

The Other Side of Truth by Beverley Naidoo

1 What two main tenses does Naidoo use in this section, and why?

2 Are all the events happening at this moment in the story?

3 What insight do we get into Sade's thoughts and feelings?

How does it work?

Naidoo uses juxtaposition to place past events next to present ones in Sade's mind. This indicates her confusion at this moment in time, and the trauma she has suffered.

Now you try it

Now look at the mini-saga 'Like Mother, Like Son'.

1955

Dear Mummy,
I hate this boarding school. Food awful, prefects bully me.
Please take me home.
    Love, David

Dear David,
Nonsense! Chin up.
    Mother

1997

Dear David,
I hate this Home. Food awful, nurses treat me like a child.
Fetch me immediately.
    Mother

Dear Mother,
Nonsense! Chin up.
    David

'Like Mother, Like Son' by Pauline Cartledge,
The Daily Telegraph, 3 May 1997

4 How does the writer use time patterns and repetitions to

a) suggest developments in plot

b) create a link between past and present

c) convey a moral?

Apply your skills

5 Write two paragraphs analysing how the two writers juxtapose present and past.

Consider the effect created by this juxtaposition, and think about why the authors have chosen to write in this way.

Top tip

When considering the *effect* of a piece of writing, think about the kind of tone that is created (for example, is it serious or humorous?) and whether this makes the reader empathise with the characters.

Check your progress

Some progress

I can recognise a few ways in which a writer organises and structures a text.

Good progress

I can comment on how writers structure a text and use juxtaposition to shape meaning in a text.

Excellent progress

I can discuss the effects of writers' choices in organising and structuring a text, and in using juxtaposition to shape meaning.

Compare the organisation and development of a theme through a whole text

Learning objective

• compare the ways in which ideas are organised in two different texts.

The way a poet organises the layout and structure of a poem can help him or her develop a theme. You can see the effect of such organisation by comparing two poems on the same theme.

Getting you thinking

Read this **sonnet**.

Remember

Remember me when I am gone away,
    Gone far away into the silent land;
    When you can no more hold me by the hand,
Nor I half turn to go, yet turning stay.
Remember me when no more day by day
    You tell me of our future that you plann'd:
    Only remember me; you understand
It will be late to counsel then or pray.
Yet if you should forget me for a while
    And afterwards remember, do not grieve:
    For if the darkness and corruption leave
    A vestige of the thoughts that once I had,
Better by far you should forget and smile
    Than that you should remember and be sad.

Christina Rossetti

Glossary

sonnet: a 14-line poem with a fixed rhythm and rhyme that often deals with 'deep' subjects such as love and death

1 In pairs, find examples of where the poet uses the following techniques.

- *rhyme*: the echoing of a sound, usually at the end of a line of poetry

- *rhyme scheme*: the pattern of rhyme in a poem

- *enjambment*: where the end of a line of poetry is not 'stopped' by punctuation – the sentence runs over into the next line

- *repetition*: repeating words, phrases, lines, often in a pattern (as in a chorus)

2 What do these features add to the meaning and feeling of the poem?

How does it work?

The poem's regular rhyme scheme of *abbaabbacddece*, reflects the way in which the poet is trying to make sense of death. The words 'remember' and 'day' are repeated, which suggests the importance of memory and time to the poet.

Now you try it

In pairs, read this two-stanza poem by Emily Dickinson. It is not told from the perspective of the person leaving or dying, but from the person left behind.

Part Three: Love (II)

You left me, sweet, two legacies,
A legacy of love
A Heavenly Father would content,
Had He the offer of;

You left me boundaries of pain
Capacious as the sea,
Between eternity and time,
Your consciousness and me.

Emily Dickinson

3 Which words suggest that this poem is about something big and important?

4 Make a table like the one below to compare the two poems and explain the effects of each writer's choices.

Rosetti	Dickinson
First person account	
Sonnet form	
Regular rhythm: **iambic pentameter**	
Full rhymes at the end of lines	
Theme of lost love	

Apply your skills

5 Write up your findings from the above. Focus on a few key features rather than the whole list, and explain how they help to convey the poets' feelings about lost love.

Glossary

Capacious: vast, having lots of space inside

Alliteration: repetition of same or similar sounds at the beginning of words

iambic pentameter: a rhyming pattern used in poetry, in which each line has ten syllables with alternating stresses

Top Tip

Think about line lengths, enjambment and patterns like repetition and **alliteration**, and the feelings expressed.

Check your progress

Some progress

I can describe the form of a poem and comment on its use of rhyme and rhythm.

Good progress

I can understand and explain why poets choose different features such as rhyme, rhythm, enjambment and repetition.

Excellent progress

I can compare the ways in which two poets use features such as rhyme, rhythm, enjambment and repetition to shape meaning.

Check your progress

Some progress

- I understand the way in which different narrative viewpoints affect how a story is structured.
- I know how to organise and structure a whole text.
- I can discuss the ways in which a script and a poem are organised and structured.

Good progress

- I can discuss the way in which narrative viewpoint affects how a story is written and structured.
- I can discuss in detail the way in which a playscript is organised, including the effects of structural features.
- I understand how to structure and organise a whole text and how to use narrative tone.
- I can explain why writers choose different features for poems.
- I can comment on how writers organise and structure a text and use juxtaposition to shape meaning in a text.

Excellent progress

- I can explain how and why narrative viewpoint affects the way in which a story is written and structured.
- I understand how to organise and structure a whole text and how to use narrative tone and humour.
- I can discuss the effects of writers' choices in organising and structuring a text and in using juxtaposition to shape meaning.
- I can compare two playscripts, looking at organisation and structural features.
- I can compare the ways in which two poems are organised and how their features shape their meaning.

Chapter 4

Explain and comment on writers' use of language, including grammatical and literary features at word and sentence level

What's it all about?

You need to be able to explain how writers choose words and construct sentences for maximum impact.

This chapter will show you how to

- identify and comment on emotive language
- infer and comment on meaning in persuasive texts
- explain and comment on writers' use of irony
- analyse how writers use different sentence structures and rhythms
- explore different kinds of dialogue in fiction
- compare how writers use descriptive language in different texts.

Identify and comment on emotive language

Learning objective

- identify emotive language, what emotions it stirs up, and how effective it is.

Emotive language deliberately stirs up the feelings of the reader or listener. It can be used in political speeches, leaflets or essays, and in adverts that encourage people to support campaigns for change – for example, to end child poverty or cruelty to animals. It is also used in poetry.

> **Top tip**
>
> Emotive language can evoke different emotions – such as anger, guilt, sympathy or hope.

Getting you thinking

Read the poem below, written by Wilfred Owen in reaction to the day-to-day killing in World War I.

Anthem for Doomed Youth

What **passing-bells** for these who die as cattle?
Only the monstrous anger of the guns.
Only the stuttering rifles' rapid rattle
Can patter out their hasty **orisons**.
No **mockeries** now for them; no prayers nor bells,
Nor any voice of mourning save the choirs, –
The shrill, demented choirs of wailing shells;
And bugles calling for them from sad **shires**.

What candles may be held to speed them all?
Not in the hands of boys, but in their eyes
Shall shine the holy glimmers of goodbyes.
The **pallor** of girls' brows shall be their **pall**;
Their flowers the tenderness of patient minds,
And each slow dusk a drawing-down of blinds.

Wilfred Owen

 Which words and phrases in the poem do you find emotive?

How does it work?

You don't need to understand every word of this poem to get a sense of its mood, and of the kind of emotions the poet wanted to arouse.

To comment on the poem, first look at the emotive phrases and consider what the poet is suggesting.

Glossary

passing-bells: funeral bells

orisons: prayers

mockeries: ceremonies that would seem meaningless in the circumstances

shires: counties

pallor: paleness

pall: funeral sheet

Emotive word or phrase	What it suggests
'die as cattle'	This image suggests that the men are treated as if they are no more important than cattle, and have as little choice in their fate.
'monstrous anger of the guns'	This image makes the guns themselves sound angry, hinting at the aggression that has caused the war; 'monstrous' suggests something huge, ugly and immoral.

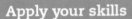

Now you try it

 2 Discuss with a partner how Wilfred Owen's choice of words in the last six lines of the poem encourages the reader to feel sad about the war.

   a) Who might the girls be, and why is there 'pallor' on their 'brows'?

   b) Why are there no flowers for the soldiers, but simply 'patient minds'?

   c) What does the 'drawing-down of blinds' suggest? Who would be drawing the blinds down 'each slow dusk'?

Apply your skills

The following poem, by Siegfried Sassoon, is about the moment when World War I ended.

Everyone Sang

Everyone suddenly burst out singing;
And I was filled with such delight
As prisoned birds must find in freedom,
Winging wildly across the white
Orchards and dark-green fields; on – on – and out of sight.

Everyone's voice was suddenly lifted;
And beauty came like the setting sun:
My heart was shaken with tears; and horror
Drifted away... O, but Everyone
Was a bird; and the song was wordless; the singing will never
   be done.

Siegfried Sassoon

Check your progress:

Some progress
I can identify emotive language.

Good progress
I can identify how emotive language arouses particular emotions.

Excellent progress
I can discuss and evaluate the effectiveness of emotive language.

 3 Write about the emotions the poem arouses in you as a reader, and how the poet's choice of words helps achieve this.

Infer and comment on meaning in persuasive texts

Learning objectives

- understand how writers use language to persuade
- infer meaning in writers' use of language, and comment on it.

A writer's word choices can persuade readers to support a particular viewpoint or to follow a course of action. To infer meaning is to work out what meaning is implied, or suggested, by the author's word choices.

Getting you thinking

Read the **propaganda** poem below, written in 1916 to encourage young British men to sign up to fight the Germans in World War I.

Glossary

propaganda: information that is intended to persuade people to do or believe something

Who's for the Game?

Who's for the game, the biggest that's played,
The red crashing game of a fight?
Who'll grip and tackle the job unafraid?
And who thinks he'd rather sit tight?
Who'll toe the line for the signal to 'Go!'?
Who'll give his country a hand?
Who wants a **turn** to himself in the show?
And who wants a seat in the stand?
Who knows it won't be a picnic – not much –
Yet eagerly shoulders a gun?
Who would much rather come back with a crutch
Than lie low and be out of the fun?
Come along, lads –
But you'll come on all right –
For there's only one course to pursue,
Your country is up to her neck in a fight,
And she's looking and calling for you.

Jessie Pope

"FALL IN"

ANSWER NOW
IN YOUR COUNTRY'S
HOUR OF NEED

1. What attitude or viewpoint is presented in the poem?

2. What is the poet implying by calling war 'the game', 'the show' and 'the fun', and asking who will 'toe the line' (as in a running race)?

3. What is implied by the contrast between active verbs like 'grip and tackle' and the ideas contained in 'sit tight', 'seat in the stand' and 'lie low'?

Glossary

turn: short performance in a variety show

4 What is the effect of the poem using questions?

5 How might clichés such as 'tackle the job' and 'won't be a picnic' help to persuade young men to join up?

How does it work?

Words and phrases have associations – ideas or judgements that readers connect with them. For example, 'grip and tackle' sounds strong and positive, but 'lie low' sounds negative – as if someone is hiding in a cowardly way. Verbs such as these, and nouns such as 'game', can be just as positive or negative as adjectives (such as 'unafraid').

Now you try it

Read the extract below from a speech by Winston Churchill, made during World War II. It encourages people to resist Hitler and the Nazis, and warns against the consequences of losing the war.

IT'S UP TO YOU

Hitler knows that he will have to break us in this island or lose the war. If we can stand up to him, all Europe may be free and the life of the world may move forward into broad, sunlit uplands. But if we fail, then the whole world, including the United States, including all that we have known and cared for, will sink into the abyss of a new Dark Age made more sinister, and perhaps more protracted, by the lights of perverted science. Let us therefore brace ourselves to our duties, and so bear ourselves that, if the British Empire and its Commonwealth last for a thousand years, men will still say, 'This was their finest hour.'

Winston Churchill, 18 June 1940

6 Look at how Churchill presents the possible outcomes of the war. Discuss how the second sentence uses positive language, including a metaphor, while the third sentence uses negative language, with a contrasting metaphor.

7 Discuss the effect of 'stand up to him'. How would 'win the war' have a different effect?

8 How does Churchill choose language to encourage people in his final sentence ('Let us...')?

Apply your skills

9 Read both texts again, then write three paragraphs explaining which one you find more convincing, and why. Comment on how the language used by Pope and Churchill might reflect how well each understood what they were writing about.

Check your progress:

Some progress »
I can identify positive and negative language.

Good progress »
I can infer meaning from a writer's word choices.

Excellent progress »»
I can compare the effects of writers' word choices.

Explain and comment on writers' use of irony

Learning objectives

- understand what irony is and how writers use it
- explain how effective writers' use of irony is.

There are two main kinds of irony. *Situational irony* is when something happens that seems especially unfair or inappropriate – for example, when someone drives over a cliff because they are trying to read a sign that says 'Danger: cliff'. The other kind, dealt with here, means saying one thing but really meaning something different.

Getting you thinking

In the extract below, the author has the six-year-old narrator, Scout, give her older brother Jem's account of a mysterious neighbour, Boo Radley – whom they have never actually seen.

> Jem gave a reasonable description of Boo: Boo was about six-and-a-half feet tall, judging from his tracks; he dined on raw squirrels and any cats he could catch, that's why his hands were blood-stained – if you ate an animal raw, you could never wash the blood off. There was a long jagged scar that ran across his face; what teeth he had were yellow and rotten; his eyes popped, and he drooled most of the time.
>
> *To Kill a Mockingbird* by Harper Lee

 1 How accurate do you think this description is likely to be? Why?

How does it work?

Harper Lee based the character of Scout on herself, so she is commenting ironically on her own naïve beliefs at the same age. Neither Scout nor Jem has ever seen Boo Radley, yet Jem thinks he knows all about him and Scout thinks that his description is 'reasonable'.

The adult Harper Lee knows that the description is unlikely to fit any real human being. The words 'reasonable' and 'dined'

Top tip

Irony in literature is often subtly humorous, although it can also be critical. Sarcasm is a heavy-handed and deliberately hurtful form of irony.

---

are clues to her ironic meaning: they are unlikely to be used by a child.

There is a serious message behind the humour: Lee is warning us against judging people on the basis of rumour.

Now you try it

Jonathan Swift was a satirist – someone who criticises others using **ridicule**. He was born in Ireland, which at the time was a very poor country ruled by Britain. His essay 'A Modest Proposal' (1729) suggests what should be done with poor children in Ireland.

I have been assured by a very knowing American of my acquaintance in London, that a young healthy child, well nursed, is at a year old a most delicious, nourishing, and wholesome food, whether stewed, roasted, baked, or boiled; and I make no doubt that it will equally serve in a **fricassée** or a **ragout**.

I do therefore humbly offer it to public consideration that [the majority of poor Irish children], at a year old, be offered in sale to the persons of quality and fortune through the kingdom; always advising the mother to let them suck plentifully in the last month, so as to render them plump and fat for a good table.

'A Modest Proposal' by Jonathan Swift

2 Discuss with a partner how Swift uses irony in this extract. What did he really think about poverty in Ireland?

3 In pairs, discuss how you think the essay criticises the British government.

Glossary

ridicule: a form of humour that makes something or someone look ridiculous

fricassée, ragout: types of meat stew

Apply your skills

4 Using the ideas from your discussion, write a short response to the following question:

How and why do you think Swift uses irony to make his point about child poverty in Ireland?

Remember to bring in examples from the text and to explain their effect in your answer.

Check your progress:

Some progress
I can identify writers' use of irony.

Good progress
I can identify and explain writers' use of irony.

Excellent progress
I can identify, explain and evaluate writers' use of irony.

Analyse how writers use different sentence structures and rhythms

Learning objective

- understand how writers use different types of sentence structure.

Writers can use short, simple sentences or more complex ones. You need to be able to identify sentence types, explain how they develop a rhythm, pace or tone, and judge their effectiveness.

Getting you thinking

Queen Elizabeth I made this speech to her army in 1588 as the soldiers prepared for war.

> My loving people, **we** have been persuaded by some, that are careful of our safety, to take heed how we commit ourselves to armed multitudes, for fear of treachery; but I assure you, I do not desire to live to distrust my faithful and loving people.
>
> Let tyrants fear; I have always so behaved myself that, under God, I have placed my chiefest strength and safeguard in the loyal hearts and good will of my subjects. And therefore I am come amongst you at this time, not as for my recreation or sport, but being resolved, in the midst and heat of the battle, to live or die amongst you all; to lay down, for my God, and for my kingdom, and for my people, my honour and my blood, even in the dust.
>
> I know I have but the body of a weak and feeble woman; but I have the heart of a king, and of a king of England, too; and think foul scorn that Parma or Spain, or any prince of Europe, should dare to invade the borders of my realms.

Glossary

we: herself ('the royal we')

Glossary

dependent clauses: a dependent clause is a group of words that contains a subject and a verb but depends on a main clause to make complete sense

main clauses: a main clause is a part of a sentence that contains both a subject and a verb that gives information about that subject; it therefore makes complete sense on its own

1 Read the speech aloud in groups, with each person reading to the next punctuation mark. Which words would you stress to make the meaning clear and achieve impact?

2 Discuss how effectively this speech would encourage loyalty.

3 What is the purpose of the semicolon near the start of the second paragraph?

4 Explain how commas are used to separate **dependent clauses** from **main clauses** in the rest of the famously moving and defiant second paragraph.

How does it work?

The punctuation of the long, impressive sentences makes their sense clear. For example, the comma before 'even in the dust' shows this is a dependent clause. Elizabeth would have paused here for effect. The semicolons indicate places where she would have paused for slightly longer, emphasising contrasting ideas, as in the final paragraph.

Now you try it

This passage is from a novel about animals seizing control of a farm.

In January there came bitterly hard weather. The earth was like iron, and nothing could be done in the fields. Many meetings were held in the big barn, and the pigs occupied themselves with planning out the work of the coming season. It had come to be accepted that the pigs, who were manifestly cleverer than the other animals, should decide all questions of farm policy, though their decisions had to be **ratified** by a majority vote. This arrangement would have worked well enough if it had not been for the disputes between Snowball and Napoleon. These two disagreed at every point where disagreement was possible. If one of them suggested sowing a bigger acreage with barley, the other was certain to demand a bigger acreage of oats, and if one of them said that such and such a field was just right for cabbages, the other would declare that it was useless for anything except roots.

Animal Farm by George Orwell

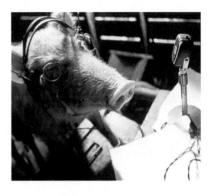

Glossary

ratified: agreed

5 With a partner, find

   a) a *simple sentence*

   b) a *compound sentence* (a sentence in which simple statements are joined by conjunctions such as 'and')

   c) a *complex sentence* (a sentence in which one or more subordinate clauses add information to a main clause).

6 The opening two sentences are short and straightforward; those about the pigs are long and complex. What does this contrast suggest?

Apply your skills

7 Write a paragraph about how Orwell uses different sentence types to introduce plot information and to compare Napoleon and Snowball.

Check your progress:

Some progress
I can see how different sentence types work grammatically.

Good progress
I can see how writers use different sentence types stylistically.

Excellent progress
I can evaluate writers' stylistic use of sentence types.

Explore different kinds of dialogue in fiction

Learning objective

- understand how authors use dialogue effectively to reveal character, relationships between characters, and feelings.

Dialogue enlivens a story, develops the plot and reveals character. Its **register** can be formal – as in a job interview – or informal, as in a casual chat with a friend. Informal speech may use **non-Standard English**. Authors have to make dialogue appear realistic, yet still ensure it is dramatically effective. You need to be able to comment on how they try to do this.

Glossary

register: the style of language used, especially how formal it is

non-Standard English: English that includes slang or dialect words and non-Standard grammar, such as 'ain't'

Getting you thinking

In this extract, some boys are doing hard labour in an outdoor desert prison. Their punishment is to dig a hole every day.

'Well, how'd you like your first hole?' asked Squid.

Stanley groaned, and the other boys laughed.

'Well, the first hole's the hardest,' said Stanley.

'No way,' said X-Ray. 'The second hole's a lot harder. You're hurting before you even get started. If you think you're sore now, just wait and see how you feel tomorrow morning, right?'

'That's right,' said Squid.

'Plus, the fun's gone,' said X-Ray.

'The fun?' asked Stanley.

'Don't lie to me,' said X-Ray. 'I bet you always wanted to dig a big hole, right? Am I right?'

Stanley had never really thought about it before, but he knew better than to tell X-Ray he wasn't right.

'Every kid in the world wants to dig a great big hole,' said X-Ray. 'To China, right?'

'Right,' said Stanley.

'See what I mean,' said X-Ray. 'That's what I'm saying. But now the fun's gone. And you still got to do it again, and again, and again.'

'Camp Fun and Games,' said Stanley.

Holes by Louis Sachar

1 Consider these questions:

a) Who is the new boy in the group?

b) What do we learn about the relationship between X-Ray and Squid?

c) How formal or informal is the boys' dialogue? Look at the vocabulary they use, and the phrases such as 'Don't lie to me.'

d) What do X-Ray's comments and use of questions reveal about his character, and his attitude towards Stanley?

e) What can you tell about Stanley's character from his responses?

How does it work?

This dialogue seems natural but it also works dramatically, suggesting character and relationships. It makes the reader think about what it must be like to have to dig a hole every day!

• Squid speaks to Stanley in a humorous, ironic way. This suggests that he takes a certain grim pleasure in knowing that Stanley won't have enjoyed digging his first hole at all.

- However, when Stanley groans, the boys laugh. This suggests that there is a sort of camaraderie between them. It is as if they are part of a club and Stanley has just joined.

- X-Ray seems to be the leader of the group. This is suggested by the way Squid backs him up, saying 'That's right.'

- The boys speak informally, using colloquial and non-Standard English: 'No way', 'kid', 'you still got' (not 'you will still have to'). Note that Americans use 'Don't lie to me' and 'Am I right?' as jokey, informal expressions, to mean something like 'Surely' and 'You must agree with me.'

Now you try it

Read this extract from *Jane Eyre*, by Charlotte Brontë. Jane's guardian, her aunt Mrs Reed, has told Jane's future headmaster that Jane is a liar, so he has given her a moralising story to read – about a girl who dies because of telling lies. Here, ten-year-old Jane speaks her mind to her aunt. John Reed is her aunt's spoilt son.

'I am not deceitful: if I were, I should say I loved you; but I declare I do not love you: I dislike you the worst of anybody in the world except John Reed; and this book about the liar, you may give to your girl, Georgiana, for it is she who tells lies, and not I.'

Mrs Reed's hands still lay on her work inactive: her eye of ice continued to dwell freezingly on mine.

'What more have you to say?' she asked, rather in the tone in which a person might address an opponent of adult age than such as is ordinarily used to a child.

That eye of hers, that voice stirred every **antipathy** I had. Shaking from head to foot, thrilled with ungovernable **excitement**, I continued—

'I am glad you are no relation of mine: I will never call you aunt again as long as I live. I will never come to see you when I am grown up; and if any one asks me how I liked you, and how you treated me, I will say the very thought of you makes me sick, and that you treated me with miserable cruelty.'

'How dare you **affirm** that, Jane Eyre?'

Glossary

antipathy: feeling of dislike

excitement: passion

affirm: state

Jane Eyre was published in 1847, during the Victorian era. Middle-class people at that time tended to speak more formally than they do today. However, this is not the only reason why the register of the dialogue is formal.

2 In pairs, discuss which words and sentence structures seem particularly formal. Why might Jane – even at the age of only ten – choose to speak formally to her aunt?

3 Rewrite the opening paragraph in an informal register, in the sort of language that someone might use today. How is its impact different?

4 Write two or more paragraphs explaining how the words spoken by Jane and her aunt, the register of those words, and the descriptive sentences in between them, show

a) their individual characters

b) their relationship

c) their feelings at this time.

Apply your skills

5 Using what you have learned from both extracts, write an answer to the following question: How can the style and register of dialogue in a novel reveal relationships between characters?

In your answer, quote one or more pieces of evidence from each extract. Explain what the quotation shows in each case.

Check your progress:

Some progress

I can see how authors use Standard and non-Standard English in dialogue.

Good progress

I can see how authors use dialogue to reveal character and relationships.

Excellent progress

I can comment on how dialogue, including its register, reveals characters' feelings and relationships.

Compare how writers use descriptive language in different texts

Writers use descriptive language in many ways – for example, in setting the scene in a novel or poem, and in travel writing or biography. You need to be able to identify the author's purpose from the language used and the details included. You also need to be able to compare different styles of description and assess how effective they are.

Getting you thinking

1 Read the two passages that follow, then select and write down phrases that vividly bring to life the place described and the writer's experience. Look especially for imagery – for instance, similes (using 'like' or 'as') and metaphors.

I was set down from the carrier's cart at the age of three; and there with a sense of bewilderment and terror my life in the village began.

The June grass, amongst which I stood, was taller than I was, and I wept. I had never been so close to grass before. It towered above me and all around me, each blade tattooed with tiger-skins of sunlight. It was knife-edged, dark, and a wicked green, thick as a forest and alive with grasshoppers that chirped and chattered and leapt through the air like monkeys.

I was lost and didn't know where to move. A tropic heat oozed up from the ground, rank with sharp odours of roots and nettles. Snow-clouds of elder-blossom banked in the sky, showering upon me the fumes and flakes of their sweet and giddy suffocation. High overhead ran frenzied larks, screaming, as though the sky were tearing apart.

Cider with Rosie by Laurie Lee

This dolls-house garden was a magic land, a forest of flowers through which roamed creatures I had never seen before. Among the thick, silky petals of each rose-bloom lived tiny, crab-like spiders that scuttled sideways when disturbed. Their small, **translucent** bodies were coloured to match the flowers they inhabited: pink, ivory, wine-red, or buttery-yellow. On the rose-stems, encrusted with green flies, lady-birds moved like newly painted toys; lady-birds pale red with large black spots; lady-birds apple-red with brown spots; lady-birds orange with grey-and-black freckles. **Rotund** and amiable, they prowled and fed among the **anaemic** flocks of greenfly. Carpenter bees, like furry, electric-blue bears, zigzagged among the flowers, growling fatly and busily. Humming-bird hawk-moths, sleek and neat, whipped up and down the paths with a fussy efficiency, pausing occasionally on speed-misty wings to lower a long, slender **proboscis** into a bloom.

My Family and Other Animals by Gerald Durrell

How does it work?

Both authors describe how a garden seemed to them as children. Both use vivid adjectives, verbs and imagery, and appeal to the senses, but there are important differences.

Laurie Lee	Gerald Durrell
Lee conveys a strong impression of a young child's experience. We see his height relative to the grass: 'It towered above me'. Lee makes the garden exotic but threatening: 'each blade tattooed with tiger-skins of sunlight' – the double metaphor here suggests a dangerous jungle. The visual adjectives in 'knife-edged, dark, and a wicked green' also convey a sense of threat.	Durrell uses adjectives and verbs to make his garden delightfully exotic but unthreatening: 'dolls-house garden', 'a magic land', 'roamed'. Instead of describing his own emotions, Durrell focuses on the garden's inhabitants, whose appearance and behaviour he describes in loving detail. Adjectives such as 'rotund' and 'amiable' show his affection for them.
Lee favours metaphors, suggesting that from the viewpoint of his three-year-old self the garden actually was a jungle.	Durrell makes more use of similes: 'like furry, electric-blue bears'. These distance him slightly from the things described.

Glossary

translucent: semi-transparent

Rotund: round

anaemic: pale and lacking in vitality

proboscis: long mouth or sucking device

Now you try it

 2 On your own, make notes in answer to the following questions.

a) How do the two authors appeal to different senses?

b) Which author uses viewpoint to create a certain amount of humour, and how?

c) Which author *anthropomorphises* animals – making them seem almost human – and what is the effect?

d) Which author do you think was a professional naturalist, and how can you tell?

Apply your skills

In the following extracts, first Samuel Pepys (1633–1703) and then John Evelyn (1620–1706) describe the Great Fire of London.

[We] saw the fire grow; and, as it grew darker, appeared more and more, and in corners and upon steeples, and between churches and houses, as far as we could see up the hill of the City, in a most horrid, **malicious**, bloody flame, not like the fine flame of an ordinary fire. [...] We stayed till, it being darkish, we saw the fire as only one entire arch of fire from this to the other side the bridge, and in a bow up the hill for an arch of above a mile long: it made me weep to see it. The churches, houses, and all on fire and flaming at once; and a horrid noise the flames made, and the cracking of houses at their ruin.

Samuel Pepys, quoted in *The Prose and Prose Writers of Britain, from Chaucer to Ruskin* by Robert Demaus (ed.), 1860

Glossary

malicious: nasty, deliberately taking pleasure in destroying something

Oh the miserable and **calamitous** spectacle! Such as haply the world had not seen since the foundation of it, nor be outdone till the **universal conflagration thereof**. All the sky was of a fiery aspect, like the top of a burning oven, and the light seen above forty miles round about for many nights. God grant mine eyes may never behold the like, now seeing above ten thousand houses all in one flame; the noise and cracking and thunder, the hurry of people, the fall of towers, houses, and churches, was like an hideous storm, and the air all about so hot and inflamed that at last one was not able to approach it.

John Evelyn, quoted in *Diary and Correspondence of John Evelyn* by H.G. Bohn, 1872

Glossary

calamitous: disastrous

the universal conflagration thereof: the end of the world

3 In small groups, imagine you are a *London News* publishing committee. You have to decide which account to recommend for publication. Decide which one you think is more vivid and exciting, and why.

Look especially for language that expresses the horror of the fire and makes it come to life by appealing to the senses.

4 Write a report for the editor of the *London News*, comparing the two accounts and explaining your choice. Don't just write all you have to say about each in turn: keep comparing them all the way through.

These phrases could be useful for comparison: 'whereas', 'by contrast', 'differs'.

To evaluate the impact of each extract (for example, how far each author appeals to the senses or chooses details well), you could use phrases like 'more/less vivid', 'specific', 'general', 'precise', 'concrete/abstract', 'direct' and 'intense'. You could sum up by saying that one or the other is 'more effective because…'.

Check your progress:

Some progress
I can identify features of descriptive writing.

Good progress
I can compare different styles of descriptive writing.

Excellent progress
I can compare descriptive styles both in features and effectiveness.

Check your progress

Some progress

☐ I can identify and comment on emotive language.

☐ I can infer meaning from word choices.

☐ I can identify examples of irony.

☐ I can comment on how authors use short sentences for dramatic effect, and how longer sentences are structured.

☐ I can identify and comment on formal and informal register in dialogue.

Good progress

☐ I can identify and comment on the relative effectiveness of emotive language.

☐ I can comment on the persuasive impact of positive and negative word associations.

☐ I can comment on the varied effects of irony.

☐ I can comment on how writers use short sentences for dramatic effect, and on how they structure longer sentences to include clauses for effect.

☐ I can explain how authors write naturalistic yet dramatic dialogue in Standard or non-Standard English.

Excellent progress

☐ I can identify and comment on how word choices and imagery contribute to emotive language.

☐ I can analyse why words have particular associations and how these can affect meaning.

☐ I can assess the effectiveness of writers' use of irony.

☐ I can comment on the ways in which writers use short sentences for dramatic effect, on how longer sentences are structured and punctuated, and on the effects of both types of sentence in a story.

☐ I can explain how authors write effective naturalistic yet dramatic dialogue, and how it reveals character and relationships.

5

Chapter 5

Identify and comment on writers' purposes and viewpoints, and the overall effect of the text on the reader

What's it all about?

You need to be able to explain the effect of the text on the reader, and how the writer achieves it.

This chapter will show you how to

- use detailed evidence from a text to identify a writer's or an artist's purpose

- identify and explain how dramatists create an effect on their audience

- explain the purpose of a text and give detailed evidence to support your points

- explain writers' viewpoints using detailed textual evidence

- understand a text's effect on the reader and explain how the writer has created it.

Use detailed evidence to identify a writer's or an artist's purpose (Part 1)

Learning objective
- analyse and respond to the range of purposes in a text.

Every text is produced for a reason. When you analyse a written text you need to act like a detective, looking for pieces of evidence that tell you why the author created it.

Getting you thinking

In U.A. Fanthorpe's poem 'Not My Best Side', the dragon, the rescued virgin and the knight pictured in Uccello's painting *St George and the Dragon* give their version of events. Here is the second stanza.

Not My Best Side

It's hard for a girl to be sure if
She wants to be rescued. I mean, I quite
Took to the dragon. It's nice to be
Liked, if you know what I mean. He was
So nicely physical, with his claws
And lovely green skin, and that sexy tail,
And the way he looked at me,
He made me feel he was all ready to
Eat me. And any girl enjoys that.
So when this boy turned up, wearing
   machinery,

On a really *dangerous* horse, to be honest
I didn't much fancy him. I mean,
What was he like underneath the hardware?
He might have acne, blackheads or even
Bad breath for all I could tell, but the
   dragon –
Well, you could see all his equipment
At a glance. Still, what could I do?
The dragon got himself beaten by the boy,
And a girl's got to think of her future.

U.A. Fanthorpe

1 The legend usually casts the dragon as the villain, the virgin as a 'damsel in distress' and St George as the saviour. What evidence can you find that the poet wants the reader to rethink this? Does the girl's point of view surprise you?

2 Choose a word or phrase that seems different from the tone of the picture. Explain to a partner why you chose that word or phrase.

How does it work?

The poet wants you to understand the scene in the picture in a more modern way, and to entertain you. She takes the historical characters from the legend of St George and uses modern language to make you see the characters as similar to yourself.

Now you try it

St George speaks the third stanza.

Glossary

Obsolescence: the ability to become out of date (in other words, to die)

sociology: the study of the development and organisation of human societies

I have diplomas in Dragon
Management and Virgin Reclamation.
My horse is the latest model, with
Automatic transmission and built-in
Obsolescence. My spear is custom-built,
And my prototype armour
Still on the secret list. You can't
Do better than me at the moment.
I'm qualified and equipped to the
Eyebrow. So why be difficult?

Don't you want to be killed and/or rescued
In the most contemporary way? Don't
You want to carry out the roles
That **sociology** and myth have designed
   for you?
Don't you realize that, by being choosy,
You are endangering job prospects
In the spear- and horse-building industries?
What, in any case, does it matter what
You want? You're in my way.

3 St George is usually cast as a knightly hero from the Age of Chivalry. He was supposed to be noble – that is, upper class, decent and polite. Find three quotations that suggest the poet wants us to rethink this view.

Apply your skills

4 Read the two extracts again.

a) Find two examples from each extract where the poet has used modern vocabulary or informal speech to make the reader look at the characters and the situation in a new way. What do these examples tell us about the attitudes of St George and the girl?

b) Explain to a partner why you have chosen these examples.

Check your progress:

Some progress
I can clearly identify the poet's main purpose.

Good progress
I can give detailed evidence for my ideas about the poet's purpose.

Excellent progress
I can analyse a poem to comment on the poet's purpose.

Use detailed evidence to identify a writer's or an artist's purpose (Part 2)

Every text is produced for a reason. Just as we examine a written text for details of word and sentence choices, we can analyse the detail in works of visual art to uncover their purposes and meanings.

Getting you thinking

This picture was painted by Jan van Eyck in 1434. No one really knows the story behind the painting, but it gives us lots of interesting clues about the couple it portrays. Over the years many people have tried to work out why the painting was created. Now it's your turn!

1 Discuss these questions with your partner:

a) What event do you think the artist was commemorating?

b) Where and why do you think the artist included himself in the painting?

c) What clues tell you these things? Use the table below to help you.

Clue	Possible meaning
The man's hand is raised	He is greeting guests
A small dog	This **symbolises** faithfulness
Shoes have been taken off	This shows that something religious is taking place
Candle burning	Represents the eye of God
Prayer beads	Show that the couple are religious
Oranges	These symbolise fertility
Chandelier	Shows that the couple is wealthy
St Margaret carved on the back of the chair	She is the patron saint of childbirth
Latin script above the mirror	It means 'Jan van Eyck was here 1434'
The couple are (sort of) holding hands	What do you think this might mean?

Glossary

symbolises: stands for (like a white dove stands for peace)

Now you try it

2 What was the artist trying to say about the event and the couple? Why do you think this?

With a partner, select five key features of this painting that support your ideas. You can use some of the 'clues' listed in the table above, or any other features you have noticed.

Apply your skills

3 Prepare a presentation explaining what you think the artist's purpose was in creating this painting. Make sure that you use all five examples from the previous activity in your presentation. Get into small groups and present your ideas to the other members of your group.

Check your progress:

Some progress
I can identify the main purpose of the painting.

Good progress
I can give detailed evidence for the purpose of the painting.

Excellent progress
I can analyse the painting to comment on its purpose.

Identify and explain how dramatists create an effect on their audience

Learning objectives

- understand how dramatists use language to create an effect on the audience
- understand how a director's or actor's choices can affect the audience.

Plays and films are also produced for a reason. The effect that the writer is trying to create will depend on *why* they are writing.

Getting you thinking

This is an extract from the play *The Taming of the Shrew* by William Shakespeare.

Petruchio has come to the Italian town of Padua to marry Kate, who is well known for having a bad temper. Kate's father has offered to pay a lot of money to the man who will marry her but Petruchio's friend, Gremio, thinks that a fortune is not enough to put up with Kate's temper.

In this extract, Petruchio is explaining to his friend why he is not scared to marry Kate. (Note: chestnuts pop when they are put in a fire.)

GREMIO	O sir, such a life, with such a wife, were strange! But will you woo this wild-cat?
PETRUCHIO	Why came I **hither** but **to that intent**? Think you a little **din** can **daunt** mine ears? Have I not in my time heard lions roar? Have I not heard the sea puff'd up with winds Rage like an angry boar **chafed** with sweat? Have I not heard great **ordnance** in the field, And heaven's **artillery** thunder in the skies? Have I not in a pitched battle heard Loud **'larums**, neighing steeds, and trumpets' clang? And do you tell me of a woman's tongue, That gives not half so great a blow to hear As will a chestnut in a farmer's fire? Tush, tush! fear boys with bugs.

Adapted from Act 1 Scene 2 of *The Taming of the Shrew* by William Shakespeare

Glossary

hither: here

to that intent: for that reason

din: noise

daunt: scare

chafed: aggravated

ordnance: guns

artillery: cannons

'larums: alarms

1 Read the passage aloud, using the glossary with definitions of the words in bold to help you understand the meaning.

2 What experiences does Petruchio claim to have had? Try to describe them using modern language.

How does it work?

By having Petruchio recount his adventures, Shakespeare *presents* him as a brave character. Petruchio is not scared of Kate's 'din' because he feels he has already endured challenging experiences. Shakespeare also hints that Petruchio is big-headed because he boasts about his past.

Now you try it

3 Identify the images that Shakespeare uses to give the audience a clear understanding of the daring things Petruchio claims to have done.

4 Copy the table below. For each image given by Shakespeare, draw the picture that it creates in your mind. In the third column, explain why the image shows that Petruchio is brave. Choose another two phrases and add them to the table.

Quotation	Picture	Effect
'heard lions roar'	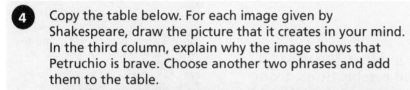	Makes Petruchio seem like a widely travelled man, who has been to dangerous and exotic places
'Rage like an angry boar'		
'heaven's artillery thunder'		

Apply your skills

An actor and a director can place their own interpretation on a character. They might choose to play up Petruchio's bravery or his boastfulness, and these different emphases will have different effects on the audience.

5 Look at the extract again with a partner. What tone should the actor playing Petruchio create for each line? Should he be boastful, angry, scornful, humorous or quiet? Use a sticky note to label each line.

Now take turns to read the passage aloud, trying to create the tone you identified.

6 Choose one of the lines and explain what effect its tone will have on the way the audience sees Petruchio.

Check your progress:

Some progress

I can identify some elements of Shakespeare's language that are intended to have an effect on the audience.

Good progress

I can explain the effect on the audience created by Shakespeare's words and the director's choices.

Excellent progress

I can understand and explain why certain language choices have the effect they do on the audience.

Explain the purpose of a text and give detailed evidence to support your points

Learning objective

- support your points with detailed evidence from the language the writer has used.

When expressing an opinion about a text, it is important that you find and use evidence to support your points.

Getting you thinking

This is the back cover 'blurb' from a book about the best festivals to go to.

> **Want to join the party?**
>
> **First-hand accounts from the festival front line.**
>
> *World Party* **is the complete guide to the world's most spectacular festivals and celebrations, from Pushkar's amazing camel fair to the carnival in Rio.**
>
> Explore every angle of over 200 events, from all over the world.
>
> Choose your festival by date, theme or country – or by chance – and plan as much, or as little, as you like.
>
> Read about the history and culture of each event, with expert insights to enrich your experience.
>
> Rely on Rough Guide's pick of the best places to stay, eat, drink and party with other festivalgoers.
>
> *World Party: The Rough Guide to the World's Best Festivals*

1 What is the *purpose* of this blurb? What evidence can you find for your answer?

Look for clues in the writer's choice of individual words and sentence structures. Think about the *type* of text this is.

How does it work?

The first sentence is a **rhetorical question** to engage the audience and it uses **ellipsis** to make it sound more like an informal conversation (the words 'Do you' have been left out). This makes it more like having a conversation with a friend than reading a formal book.

The text uses a **superlative** ('most spectacular') and **hyperbole** ('amazing') to emphasise the excitement of the book.

Glossary

rhetorical question: a question asked for effect, which is not meant to be answered

ellipsis: missing out a word or phrase that you might expect to be there

superlative: an adjective that means the most (e.g. biggest)

hyperbole: exaggeration used for effect

2 Find examples of

a) words that make this book sound as if it has been written by knowledgeable people?

b) words or short phrases that make the book sound **comprehensive**?

c) words or short phrases that make the information in the book seem trustworthy.

Now think about how the writer has structured the sentences to achieve his purpose.

3 Find these **imperative** verbs in the text:

explore   choose   read   rely

a) Where do they come in their sentences?

b) How do they suggest that the writer is reliable and able to take charge of the reader's holiday?

4 Choose one imperative and explain to your partner why it has been used.

5 Which clues tell you what kind of person the blurb is aimed at?

Glossary

comprehensive: telling you everything you need to know

imperative: a command or request (*Do* this, *Explore*)

Apply your skills

6 Now use the information you have gathered to answer this question:

Does this text achieve its purpose?

Make sure you have

- an introductory paragraph in which you say what the purpose of the text is

- at least three paragraphs making different points

- a conclusion in which you give your answer to the question.

7 Re-read your work or swap with a partner. Does the answer

- use clues to work out the *purpose* of the text?

- give precise evidence at *word* and *sentence levels* for the points

- use clues from across the *whole* text?

- explain why the text is *effective* at achieving its purpose for the target audience?

Check your progress:

Some progress

I can identify the main purpose of a text clearly.

Good progress

I can give evidence for the purpose of a text by looking at the writer's word choices, sentence structures and whole-text organisation.

Excellent progress

I can comment on a writer's purposes analytically.

Explain writers' viewpoints using detailed textual evidence

Learning objective

- develop your skills in understanding and explaining the viewpoint that a writer is using.

Do you always accept what people tell you without asking them to give you a reason? When you talk about texts, you need to give evidence for your ideas and explain your reasons.

Getting you thinking

Read this opening to a poem.

Noon

Noon,
      and its sacred water sprinkles.
A schoolgirl in blue and white uniform,
her golden plaits a simple **coronet**
out of **Angelico**, a fine sweat on her forehead,
hair where the twilight singed and signed its **epoch**.

Derek Walcott

1 With a partner, make a list of the things that we are told about the girl.

2 Next to each one, write down what you think the poet wants us to deduce from this information.

For example, you could start:

> She looks like a character from a religious painting.
> She is being shown as like an angel.

Glossary

coronet: a small crown

Angelico: an artist who painted religious subjects such as angels

epoch: an important period in someone's life

How does it work?

This poem is written in the *third* person. The narrator of the poem describes the girl as if he is watching her. He gives us a lot of information about what he thinks of her. Details like 'a simple coronet' and the 'fine' sweat on her forehead suggest that the poem is narrated from the *viewpoint* of someone who loves or admires her.

Now you try it

Now read the next part of the poem.

> And a young man going home.
> They move away from each other.
> They are moving towards each other.
> His head roars with hunger and poems.
> His hand is trembling to recite her name.

3 Write down two things that we learn about this young man's feelings. Which words tell you how he feels?

4 Do you understand more about his feelings or about the schoolgirl's? Write a paragraph explaining your answer to this question. Use examples from the text.

Apply your skills

5 With a partner, read the whole poem aloud. One of you should read the lines that focus on the girl, and the other those that give us the viewpoint of the boy. Afterwards, discuss which words and phrases made you choose who read which lines.

> Noon,
>   and its sacred water sprinkles.
> A schoolgirl in blue and white uniform,
> her golden plaits a simple coronet
> out of Angelico, a fine sweat on her forehead,
> hair where the twilight singed and signed its epoch.
> And a young man going home.
> They move away from each other.
> They are moving towards each other.
> His head roars with hunger and poems.
> His hand is trembling to recite her name.
> She clutches her books, she is laughing,
> her uniformed companions laughing.
> She laughs till she is near tears.

6 Explain the overall viewpoint of the writer. How does he feel about the two characters in the poem? (Remember that the viewpoint might change or develop over the course of the poem.) You need to give your reasons for this interpretation, and to find evidence in the text to support your ideas.

Check your progress:

Some progress

I can clearly identify the writer's viewpoint and explain my ideas.

Good progress

I can explain the writer's viewpoint using detailed reference to the text.

Excellent progress

I can comment analytically on the way in which the writer establishes viewpoint in the text.

Understand a text's effect on the reader and explain how the writer has created it

All texts have an effect on you as a reader. For example, they can make you like or hate a person or place that is described. These effects are created through the writer's choice of imagery, words, punctuation and organisation of paragraphs, lines and stanzas.

Getting you thinking

Read this poem.

Midsummer, Tobago

Broad sun-stoned beaches.

White heat.
A green river.

A bridge,
scorched yellow palms

from the summer-sleeping house
drowsing through August.

Days I have held,
days I have lost,

days that outgrow, like daughters,
my **harbouring** arms.

Derek Walcott

The writer uses images to build up a picture of the place. He doesn't need to use many words because he has chosen them so carefully.

1. Look at the first seven lines of the poem. With a partner, choose pictures from the Internet to illustrate each image in these lines.

2. Make a collage of the images in the poem, annotating each one with words or phrases from the poem to build up the picture that the poet creates in our minds.

3. What do these images tell you about the place that Walcott is describing?

Glossary

harbouring: protecting, giving safety

How does it work?

Walcott uses a list of images to create a sense of a sleepy and slow place in the reader's mind. It feels like the days will last forever, but in reality they drift away and time moves on, just as if the daughters who have grown up and no longer need his protection.

Now you try it

4 Copy out and annotate two stanzas from the poem to show the effects that Walcott creates through his use of language.

Think about the following features:

- punctuation choices
- length of lines and words
- sounds the poet has chosen
- adjectives and use of colour
- alliteration.

One has been done for you as an example.

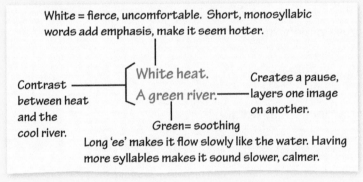

Apply your skills

5 How does Derek Walcott make the reader feel about midsummer in Tobago in the first seven lines? Consider

a) the effect of the poem on the reader – how it makes the reader feel

b) the way Walcott uses words and phrases

c) the way he uses punctuation

d) how effective you think these lines are.

6 Now use all your notes and examples to answer these questions.

- What effect has the poem had on you as a reader?
- How was this effect achieved?

Check your progress:

Some progress

I can explain what effect a text has on the reader.

Good progress

I can identify the effect of a text on the reader and say how it has been created.

Excellent progress

I can explain how a writer uses techniques and devices to achieve an effect.

Check your progress

Some progress

- [ ] I can identify what the writer is trying to achieve (the writer's purpose).
- [ ] I can identify the writer's viewpoint.
- [ ] I can identify the effect a text has on the reader.
- [ ] I can explain my ideas.

Good progress

- [ ] I can clearly explain the purpose of a text.
- [ ] I can clearly explain the viewpoint of the writer or persona in more complex texts.
- [ ] I can clearly identify the effect on the reader and say how that effect has been created.
- [ ] I can give detailed evidence for my opinions at word level.
- [ ] I can give detailed evidence for my opinions at sentence level.
- [ ] I can give detailed evidence for my opinions at whole-text level.

Excellent progress

- [ ] I can analyse a text to explain the writer's purpose.
- [ ] I can evaluate how the writer's viewpoint develops across a whole text.
- [ ] I can explain how the writer has used language to achieve the effect that he or she intended.

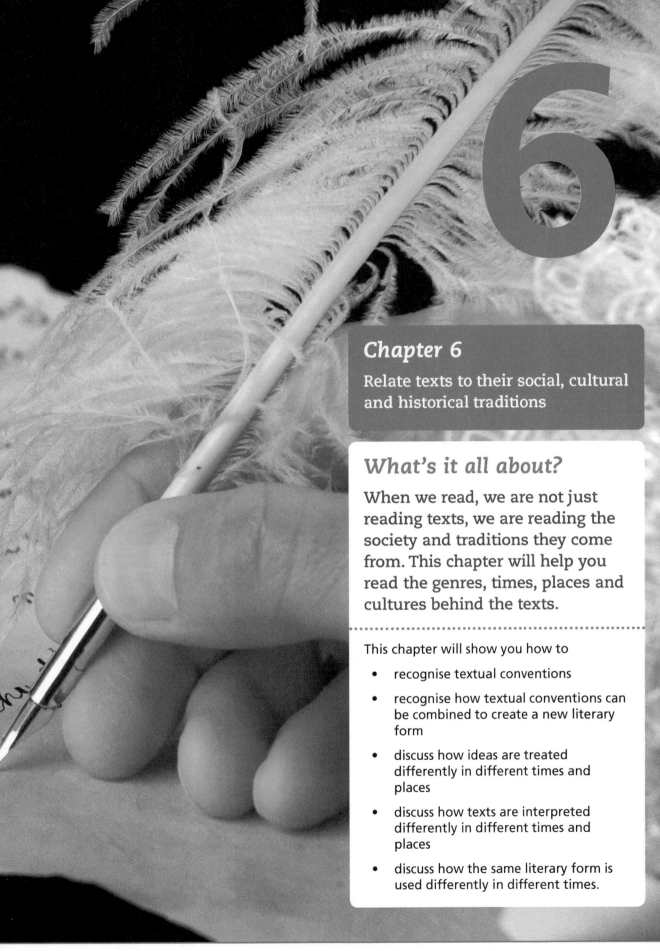

Chapter 6

Relate texts to their social, cultural and historical traditions

What's it all about?

When we read, we are not just reading texts, we are reading the society and traditions they come from. This chapter will help you read the genres, times, places and cultures behind the texts.

This chapter will show you how to

- recognise textual conventions
- recognise how textual conventions can be combined to create a new literary form
- discuss how ideas are treated differently in different times and places
- discuss how texts are interpreted differently in different times and places
- discuss how the same literary form is used differently in different times.

Recognise textual conventions

Learning objectives

- explore some of the conventions of travel writing
- understand the difference between Standard and non-Standard English.

Each form of writing has its own rules – called conventions. One convention of travel writing is the familiar made strange, where something familiar to the reader is seen through an outsider's eyes.

Getting you thinking

> It was about the beginning of the spring 1757 when I arrived in England, and I was near twelve years of age at that time. I was very much struck with the buildings and the pavement of the streets in Falmouth; and, indeed, any object I saw filled me with new surprise. One morning, when I got upon deck, I saw it covered all over with the snow that fell overnight: as I had never seen any thing of the kind before, I thought it was salt; so I immediately ran down to the mate, and desired him, as well as I could, to come and see how somebody in the night had thrown salt all over the deck. He, knowing what it was, desired me to bring some of it down to him: accordingly I took up a handful of it, which I found very cold indeed; and when I brought it to him he desired me to taste it. I did so, and I was surprised beyond measure.
>
> *The Interesting Narrative* by Olaudah Equiano

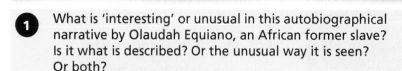

Olaudah Equiano,
or
GUSTAVUS VASSA,
the African?

1 What is 'interesting' or unusual in this autobiographical narrative by Olaudah Equiano, an African former slave? Is it what is described? Or the unusual way it is seen? Or both?

How does it work?

White Europeans might find Equiano's first experience of snow more 'interesting' than what he sees. However, others might share his fascination with snow, Western buildings and pavements. Good travel writing turns all readers into 'outsiders' – seeing the thing described with fresh eyes.

Now you try it

The following extract gives an immigrant's view of London in 1956. The narrator tells the story of the 'Windrush' generation newly arrived from the West Indies.

With that, Moses start shining his shoes, and Sir Galahad went out to try and get a work.

Galahad make for the tube station when he left Moses, and he stand there on Queensway watching everybody going about their business, and a feeling of loneliness and fright come on him all of a sudden. He forget all the brave words he was talking to Moses, and he realize that here he is, in London, and he ain't have money or work or place to sleep or any friend or anything, and he standing up here by the tube station watching people, and everybody look so busy he frighten to ask questions from any of them. You think any of them bothering with what going on in his mind? Or in anybody else mind but their own? He see a test come and take a newspaper and put down the money on a box – nobody there to watch the fellar and yet he put the money down. What sort of thing is that? Galahad wonder, they not afraid somebody thief the money?

The Lonely Londoners by Sam Selvon

2 In pairs, decide what is happening here. What does the narrator observe, and why does he think it is strange?

3 Where is the language itself non-Standard English? Look for *dialect* vocabulary such as 'a work' (a job) and non-Standard grammar such as 'he ain't have money' (he has no money), 'he stand' (he stands) and 'they not afraid' (they're not afraid).

Apply your skills

The writer first wrote this book in Standard English and then in **Creole**, but neither worked – until he mixed both.

4 Rewrite a few lines of the passage in Standard English. What is lost by doing this?

Glossary

Creole: a language that has developed from a mixture of two other languages in places where groups of people did not speak a common language

Check your progress:

Some progress
I can give some explanation of the difference between non-Standard and Standard English.

Good progress
I can discuss in detail the difference between non-Standard and Standard English.

Excellent progress
I can analyse the difference between non-Standard and Standard English.

Recognise how textual conventions can be combined to create a new literary form

Learning objectives

- tell the difference between different types of literary text
- understand the different conventions of particular texts.

Different texts have different conventions. These conventions can be about a text's language, structure and ideas, or about its appearance and presentation. A major part of a text's meaning depends on its form: is it fiction or not – and if so, what kind?

Getting you thinking

Look at the extract below. An Italian duke is showing a visitor around his private art gallery. He is wealthy and powerful – and evidently above the law. He is used to getting his own way, especially with his wives.

All of this is revealed by the duke's own words to his guest about a painting of his 'last' wife, which was done by an artist called Frà Pandolf.

My Last Duchess

That's my last Duchess painted on the wall,
Looking as if she were alive;
          [...] Sir, 'twas not
Her husband's presence only, called that spot
Of joy into the Duchess' cheek: perhaps
Frà Pandolf chanced to say 'Her **mantle** laps
Over my Lady's wrist too much,' or 'Paint
Must never hope to reproduce the faint
Half-flush that dies along her throat': such stuff
Was **courtesy**, she thought, and cause enough
For calling up that spot of joy. She had
A heart ... how shall I say? ... too soon made glad,
Too easily impressed; she liked whate'er
She looked on, and her looks went everywhere.
    [...] She thanked men, – good; but thanked
Somehow ... I know not how ... as if she ranked
My gift of **a nine hundred years old name**
With anybody's gift.
    [...] This grew; I gave commands;
Then all smiles stopped together. There she stands
As if alive. Will't please you rise? We'll meet
The company below, then.

Glossary

mantle: a loose wrap or cloak

courtesy: politeness

a nine hundred years old name: he's from an ancient aristocratic family

1 Do you think this extract is from a newspaper, poem, history textbook, novel, advertisement, play, travel book or something else?

How does it work?

The text has several *conventions* that we expect of literature:

- It is written in *verse*.
- A person or *character* (Ferrara), who doesn't seem to be the writer, is speaking to us and we are being told a story.

History textbooks and newspapers have other conventions – for example, a less personal tone and a greater use of factual information. They would tell the same story in different ways.

Now you try it

2 Find any evidence that makes you think it is

a) a *play* (Does it have a character? Someone who seems to be speaking to someone else? Is it set out like a play?)

b) a *poem* (Does it use lines of verse, or sound effects like rhymes?)

c) a *story* (Does it use a 'made-up' character? Does it have a narrator?).

3 What exactly happens in the text? List the events of the Duke's story in the order he reports them to his listener.

Use this observation as a starting point.

> He says his wife liked the attention of other men
> (it says 'twas not / Her husband's presence only,
> called that spot / Of joy into the Duchess' cheek').

4 What do you think (or imagine) Ferrara has done to his 'last' Duchess?

Apply your skills

So, is this a story, play or poem? In fact, 'My Last Duchess' is all three – and none – of them at the same time! It is a form called a dramatic monologue, developed by the Victorian poet Robert Browning.

5 Write a paragraph, using examples from 'My Last Duchess' to explain

a) how dramatic monologue works

b) what conventions it includes.

Check your progress:

Some progress
I can identify a dramatic monologue.

Good progress
I can identify a dramatic monologue and explore some of its features.

Excellent progress
I can analyse a dramatic monologue and explore its development as a literary form.

Discuss how ideas are treated differently in different times and places

Learning objective

- relate ideas in texts to the changing attitudes of our own society.

The way we read texts is influenced by our time and place of reading, and by the values of our own society.

Getting you thinking

In the following extract, an African slave boy is about to die.

> Sarah straightened up, her face full of suppressed anger. 'You can make a big parade of your feelings over this,' she snapped. '[...] You can attend the funeral, you can hire a hearse. It is throwing bad money after good. The child is dying, and you knew when you started this that at least two or three would die during the first year. It is natural wastage. It is the natural loss of **stock**. If we have to go into mourning every time a slave dies we might as well grieve for a broken barrel of sugar.'
>
> 'He is a child,' Frances cried passionately. 'A little boy...'
>
> 'He is our Trade,' Sarah said. 'And if we cannot make this Trade pay then we are on the way to ruin. Wear black crepe if you like, Sister. But get those slaves trained and ready for sale.'
>
> *A Respectable Trade* by Philippa Gregory

Glossary

stock: livestock, such as cattle or sheep

 Whose side are you on, Frances's or Sarah's?

How does it work?

In this extract, modern readers will almost certainly side with Frances. A human child is dying. We are unlikely to read this tragedy as 'a natural loss of stock' or a 'broken barrel of sugar'.

However, in Bristol in the 1780s, when this story is set, many people – including those who could be kind and thoughtful in other ways – might have sided with Sarah. That society valued the (African) Trade for its slaves and the West Indian sugar, coffee, tobacco and rum that it produced. With the exception of those in the growing anti-slave movement, people in this society did not value the human life of an African slave – except as livestock, valued at about £50 per head.

Modern readers will read this extract from a completely different social context, one in which people are appalled by the slave trade.

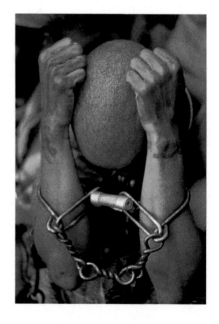

2 In pairs, discuss the following questions.

a) Can you remember anything that you wore last weekend?

b) Were you, or was the person who bought your clothes, pleased with the 'bargain' price? Or perhaps the 'label'?

c) Are you pleased with the quality, fit and style?

d) Do you know where – or how – the clothes were made?

3 In your pairs, imagine it is 2050. This society makes it illegal to

- pay developing-world factory owners less than a fair price for the materials they produce

- pay workers less than a reasonable living wage

- buy or sell animal products, such as leather or furs, as clothing for humans.

Now read the following advertisements from our own time.

## Autumn collection now in store! Subscribe to Cool Fashions Newsletter and receive the latest fashion news and fantastic offers. The brightest fabrics from Asia and Africa at a fraction of the price. And as a thank you, we will give you a welcome coupon of 20% to use on your next purchase.	## Winter Sale *Absolutely All SALE Items Half Price or Even Less* Leather.co.uk – shop online for the latest leather fashion. Heat-retaining but great-looking leather garments and snug-as-a-fox furs that fit like your own skin. Keep warm – and stay minky cool!

How do you think the society in 2050 would view these 'old' adverts? Discuss this question in role, as if you have just come across these adverts from 2014.

> **Top tip**
>
> Just as we 'read' the slave trade context differently from people in the 1780s, a future society might read *our* shopping habits differently.

Check your progress:

> **Some progress** »
> I can give some explanation of how texts are read differently in different times.

> **Good progress** »»
> I can explore in some detail how texts are read differently in different times.

> **Excellent progress** »»»
> I can analyse how texts are read differently in different times.

4 Individually, write up your thoughts on

a) why attitudes to texts change over time

b) whether texts from previous times should still be read today, even if they show values different from our own.

Discuss how texts are interpreted differently in different times and places

Learning objective

- understand how the same text can be reinterpreted.

The way in which people read and reinterpret texts is influenced by their time and place of reading, and the values of their own society.

Getting you thinking

Read this extract from a tale published in 1818. A doctor has just created a living monster after years of trying to do so.

> It was on a dreary night of November that I beheld the accomplishment of my toils. With an anxiety that almost amounted to agony, I collected the instruments of life around me, that I might infuse a spark of being into the lifeless thing that lay at my feet. It was already one in the morning; the rain pattered dismally against the panes, and my candle was nearly burnt out, when, by the glimmer of the half-extinguished light, I saw the dull yellow eye of the creature open; it breathed hard, and a convulsive motion agitated its limbs [...] His yellow skin scarcely covered the work of muscles and arteries beneath; his hair was of a lustrous black, and flowing; his teeth of a pearly whiteness; but these luxuriances only formed a more horrid contrast with his watery eyes [...] I had worked hard for nearly two years, for the sole purpose of **infusing** life into an **inanimate** body. For this I had deprived myself of rest and health. I had desired it with an **ardour** that far exceeded moderation; but now that I had finished, the beauty of the dream vanished, and breathless horror and disgust filled my heart. Unable to endure the aspect of the being I had created, I rushed out of the room and continued a long time traversing my bed-chamber, unable to compose my mind to sleep.

Frankenstein by Mary Shelley

1 What are the doctor's feelings as he looks on his creation?

2 Do you think the writer wants readers to share the doctor's point of view? Why or why not?

Glossary

infusing: putting, filling

inanimate: lifeless

ardour: passion

How does it work?

The early 19th century was an era of great advances in science, which made many people question long-held religious beliefs. In her novel, Shelley imaginatively explored ideas about whether scientists should 'play God' – and what the consequences might be if they did so.

This part of Mary Shelley's text is narrated from the point of view of the doctor, Victor Frankenstein. His strong – even surprising – emotions are described first. Elsewhere in the novel, Shelley tells the story from other viewpoints – including that of the creature. In the 20th century, film versions of the story usually ignored the creature's viewpoint and showed only the 'monstrous' aspect of it.

Now you try it

 3   In pairs, read and then act out this modern stage adaptation. Take turns to play Frankenstein and his creation.

> *The Creature plays with a kettle, sitting on the floor. He chews it and bangs it.*
>
> *The Creature spins like a top, on his tailbone, pushing himself round and round and round. And round and round some more.*
>
> *He stands, and is dizzy. He falls over. He laughs.*
>
> *A man is approaching slowly and cautiously: Victor Frankenstein, late twenties. He wears a long cloak. He watches the Creature intently.*
>
> *Victor goes close to the Creature, who doesn't see him at first. Victor is curious, but then repulsed by the filthy, slimy being sprawled in front of him.*
>
> *The Creature turns and sees Victor. He reaches out to him, babbling incoherently. He gives a ghastly smile. Victor is appalled. He backs off.*
>
> *The Creature pursues Victor, moving swiftly across the floor.*
>
> VICTOR   No...keep away...no...
>
> *Frankenstein* by Nick Dear

Apply your skills

 4   Write a paragraph explaining how you think Dear's stage version of the text asks us to rethink the 1818 novel. Consider

- how Dear deals with and reacts against the film versions of Frankenstein that Shelley's original readership would not have seen
- the textual differences between a 19th-century novel and a modern play
- how Mary Shelley's ideas about the ethics of science might be relevant today (think about modern scientific advances such as cloning and DNA profiling).

Check your progress:
....

Some progress ≫
I understand how texts are interpreted differently through time.

Good progress ⟫
I can explain how texts are interpreted differently through time.

Excellent progress ⟫⟫
I can describe in some detail how a text might be interpreted in different forms and in relation to its society and time.

Discuss how the same literary form is used differently in different times

Learning objective

- recognise different types of sonnets.

Literature isn't just 'made up' by every new writer that comes along. Most writers inherit what has gone before, but then use this in their own way and in the new context of their own time.

Getting you thinking

If you were serious about your feelings for someone, how would you tell them?

Traditionally, writers have used a poetic form called the 'sonnet' as a way of expressing love. Shakespeare wrote a series of 154 sonnets to a fair young man and a 'dark lady'. Here is one of them.

> My mistress' eyes are nothing like the sun;
> Coral is far more red than her lips' red;
> If snow be white, why then her breasts are **dun**;
> If hairs be wires, black wires grow on her head. 4
> I have seen roses **damasked**, red and white,
> But no such roses see I in her cheeks;
> And in some perfumes is there more delight
> Than in the breath that from my mistress reeks. 8
> I love to hear her speak, yet well I know
> That music hath a far more pleasing sound;
> I grant I never saw a goddess go;
> My mistress when she walks treads on the ground. 12
>   And yet, by heaven, I think my love as rare
>   As any **she** belied with false compare. 14
>
> William Shakespeare

Glossary

dun: a light muddy-brown colour

damasked: richly patterned

she (line 14): woman

It was a convention of the sonnets of Shakespeare's time to compare a woman to beautiful objects in nature. Here, Shakespeare plays with this idea to create an original and seemingly more sincere sonnet.

 1 In groups of four, take one section each (lines 1–4; 5–8; 9–12; 13–14) and read it closely. Then work together to answer the following questions.

a) Lines 1–12: How is the girl not like sunshine, roses, music and so on?

b) Lines 13–14: How, according to Shakespeare, is she better than the usual love object?

The first sonnet – the Italian formation 8, 6 – was invented by the Florentine poet Petrarch (1304–1374) to praise (and blame) his lady-love Laura. He called it a sonneto (a 'little song').

Sir Thomas Wyatt brought the sonnet back to the English court during Henry VIII's reign and soon everyone was writing the fashionable new poem 'for the ladies'. The English formation – 4, 4, 4, 2 – developed because it offers more rhyme choices. (It's easier to rhyme in Italian than in English.)

Both forms of the sonnet have 14 lines, a strict rhyme scheme, and divide into clear sections. However, there are some important differences.

Italian/Petrarchan sonnet	English/Shakespearean sonnet
In the Italian sonnet, there is a *turn* in the poem after line 8, reinforced by a new pattern of rhymes in lines 9–14.	In the English sonnet, there is a *final couplet* where the argument is clinched, extended or reversed in a dramatic way.
The Italian sonnet is '*a poem of two halves*' split into eight lines and six lines. The second part 'rejects' the first (8, 6).	The English sonnet also has two halves but the rhyme patterns divide into 12 (3 linked quatrains) and 2 (a couplet that briefly summarises and contrasts).
In the Italian version, the *rhymes* (and sometimes the layout) mark a clear break between the first half and the second.	The English version repeats a four-line idea three times and then 'turns' in the conclusion. The *rhyme scheme* (ABAB CDCD EFEF GG) reflects this.
The Italian version complains for eight lines, then turns and accepts that love is worth it.	The English can love and complain at the same time!

Now you try it

Two hundred years later, the poet Wordsworth returns to Petrarch's original form – eight lines 'answered' by six – but changes the content. His 'little song' describes a passenger leaving Revolutionary France, a black woman deported by new laws.

September 1, 1802

We had a fellow-Passenger who came
From Calais with us, **gaudy in array**,
A Negro Woman like a Lady gay,
Yet silent as a woman fearing blame;
Dejected, meek, yea pitiably tame,
She sate, from notice turning not away,
But on our **proffer'd** kindness still did lay
A weight of **languid** speech, or at the same
Was silent, motionless in eyes and face.
She was a Negro Woman driv'n from France,
Rejected like all others of that race,
Not one of whom may now find footing there;
This the poor Out-cast did to us declare,
Nor murmur'd at the unfeeling **Ordinance**.

William Wordsworth

Glossary

gaudy in array: wearing brightly coloured clothes

proffer'd: offered

languid: weary (all hope gone)

Ordinance: law

2 What is different about the *content* or *focus* of this sonnet compared with Petrarch's and Shakespeare's?

3 In pairs, discuss the following questions.

a) What words sum up the woman's state of mind?

b) What is the woman's reaction to the law that made her leave France? Is the poet's reaction different?

4 This poem uses a 400-year-old form to express a news item (the deportation of free black people from France) in 1802.

a) Why does Wordsworth use a 'love poem' form to write about this subject?

b) Can you find two 'halves' formed by rhyme patterns?

c) The poem is in two sentences. Do they match with the two rhyme sections?

5 Now look at the poem's language. Wordsworth's poem is over two centuries old – which words are outdated, altered, quaint or even offensive to a modern reader? Explain why.

6 Write a comparison of the two sonnets by Shakespeare and Wordsworth. Comment on

a) their *purpose* (Why was each sonnet written? Is one more or less suited to the sonnet form? Why?)

b) their *form* (What features do they have in common? What features are different? What would (a) Petrarch and (b) Shakespeare recognise as a sonnet in Wordsworth's poem?)

You could use these prompts to help you structure your response:

> The fourteen-line sonnet has been popular in English literature since Tudor times. The form varies and there are different patterns of rhymes: the [type of sonnet] sonnet is rhymed… whereas the [type of sonnet] sonnet is rhymed…
>
> The sonnet was originally a love song, but it has since been used for such subjects as…
>
> In Sonnet 130, Shakespeare writes about…
>
> In 'September 1, 1802', Wordsworth writes about…
>
> Petrarch would/would not recognise Shakespeare's/ Wordsworth's poem as a sonnet because…

> **Top tip**
>
> Poets don't always obey the rules!

Check your progress:

Some progress 〉

I can compare sonnet conventions from different periods.

Good progress 〉〉

I can explore and explain sonnet conventions from different periods.

Excellent progress 〉〉〉

I can analyse two examples from the sonnet tradition.

Check your progress

Some progress

- [ ] I can compare and contrast conventions in texts.
- [ ] I can identify texts in context (times, places and social settings).
- [ ] I can make some explanation of how contexts (time, place and social settings) affect how texts are read.
- [ ] I can identify how a conventional form is used differently at different times.

Good progress

- [ ] I can recognise textual conventions in a literary form.
- [ ] I can recognise textual conventions in a non-literary form.
- [ ] I can discuss in some detail how the same literary form is used differently in different periods.
- [ ] I can discuss in some detail how the meaning of the same text can change over time.
- [ ] I can discuss in some detail how ideas in texts are interpreted differently in different times and places.

Excellent progress

- [ ] I can begin to analyse how texts are influenced by their literary tradition.
- [ ] I can begin to analyse how texts are influenced by the context in which they are written.
- [ ] I can begin to analyse how texts are influenced by the context in which they are read.
- [ ] I can begin to analyse how a text is interpreted in relation to its society, culture and time.

7

Chapter 7

Longer texts and reading activities

What's it all about?

You need to be able to bring all your reading skills together to work on longer texts.

Dreams of Anne Frank
by Bernard Kops

EDITH   Where are you going, darling?

ANNE   I need fresh air. I need to escape. I need to see my beautiful city. Just once more. I need to stretch and breathe the sky.

EDITH   (*humouring her*) Yes, darling. Don't we all.

Anne tries the trapdoor.

Darling. What are you doing?

ANNE   The empty ballroom of dreams. (*She sings.*)
Dancing in the dark till the tune ends,
We're dancing in the dark – and it soon ends –
We're waltzing in the wonder of why we're here –
Time hurries by – we're here and gone...

Anne floats into an empty square. Amsterdam at night. There are searchlights and the crump of bombs.

Come, bombs! Come, fire! Devour the Nazi monster. Even destroy my beloved Amsterdam if you have to.

Outside Inside
Outside inside
Two worlds apart
Inside we argue
Outside we part
Inside we're safe
But we fight for a chair
Outside we're taken
To God knows where
Outside inside
Two worlds apart
Inside we argue
Outside the broken heart
And sky and travel and death

*Outside the Royal Palace. A man (**Dussel**) stalks her.*

MAN   What are you doing in the streets, child? In the middle of the night?

ANNE   Looking for my childhood.

MAN   But surely you want to grow up?

ANNE   Yes. But I'm afraid. I want life to go backwards.

MAN Ah yes, I thought you were in pain. Can I tell you about my hobby? I am totally obsessed with military bands. I would follow any band, good or bad, to the ends of the earth and often do in my imagination. As soon as I get home I immediately start the military music on my radiogram. I know every march ever written, almost every band that ever played, their particular style. There in my living-room I march, back and forth, back and forth, every lunch-time, every night. It is a wonderful exercise and I can assure you it is a morally uplifting and spiritual experience. The Germans are a humane race, compassionate. I know you are afraid because of the things you have heard they have done or are about to do. A lot of this you can disregard. It is propaganda. I maintain that soon you will notice a big change. An occupying power is bound to take actions that seem draconian and excessively harsh early on. The Jews are merely an expediency, a scapegoat for our ambitions. It is almost understandable, even if a little painful. Open up. (*He has become Hitler and wants to probe into Anne's mouth.*) Where's my scalpel?

ANNE Here!

She takes the knife from his white coat pocket, thrusts it into his stomach.

1 When Anne emerges through the trapdoor, which two stage directions make it clear that Amsterdam is a city at war?

2 Would you describe this play as realistic? Consider

- the role of song/music
- the appearance and behaviour of the man (Dussel)
- how Anne behaves
- the title of the play and how it relates to what happens.

3 Why is the man's long speech important to this scene as a whole? Consider

- how he changes as it progresses
- the underlying message about the 'actions' that the Germans are taking towards Jewish people.

4 Comment on the writer's overall viewpoint in this scene. What do you think he is trying to say about

- childhood
- the effect of the war on ordinary people?

5 To what extent is the play's success dependent on the audience's knowledge of the events of World War II and of the fact that Anne Frank was a real person? Write two paragraphs explaining your point of view.

The Brooke donkey charity leaflet

The Brooke urgently needs your help to save working animals from suffering – and help the poor families who depend on them too. Right now, millions of animals carry heavy loads, such as building materials and produce. Without their help, poor families struggle to earn a living, but many don't know how to care for their donkeys and horses properly.

The Brooke's local experts treat animals when they are sick or injured – and educate owners in better animal care, saving donkeys and horses from terrible pain.

For your FREE inspiration pack and DVD, showing our work in action, visit www.helpboth.org, fill in the form below or text 'BROOKE G' to 80010*

* Each message sent to us is charged at your standard network SMS rate only. Reply STOP at any time to opt out of receiving FREE information about the Brooke, but we don't spam!

The animal charity that helps people too
The Brooke
Founded by Dorothy Brooke in 1934

Title _____

Name _____

Surname _____

Address _____

_____

_____

Postcode _____

Tel _____

Email _____

Please write your email address above if you would be happy to receive emails from the Brooke about our activities and work with animals overseas (you can unsubscribe easily at any time).

1. What two roles does the Brooke charity have? Make sure you find appropriate quotations to support your answer.

2. The leaflet implies a number of things about how charities work best – what do you think these are, and do you agree?

3. How well does the structure of the leaflet work? Comment in particular on

   - the organisation of the text into paragraphs
   - the order in which your eye is drawn to particular words or sections of text
   - the differences in how the text is presented throughout the leaflet.

4. Comment on the ways the writer uses language to achieve a particular effect.

   Consider

   - the style and tone of the text
   - any features of persuasive language that are used in the text.

   Make sure you include carefully selected quotations or references to support your point of view.

5. 'The text as a whole has several purposes, but this is a weakness as much as a strength'. Comment on this statement, making detailed reference to the text.

The Woman in White by Wilkie Collins

Daylight confirmed the impression which I had felt the night before, of there being too many trees at Blackwater. The house is stifled by them. They are, for the most part, young and planted much too thickly. On a nearer view, the garden proved to be small and poor and ill-kept. I left it behind me, opened a little gate in a ring fence, and found myself in a plantation of fir trees. After a walk of about half a mile, the path took a sudden turn and I found myself suddenly on the margin of a vast open space and looking down at the Blackwater lake from which the house takes its name.

The ground shelving away below me, was all sand, with a few little heathy hillocks to break the monotony of it. The lake itself had evidently once flowed to the spot on which I stood, and had gradually been wasted and dried up to less than a third of its former size. I saw its still, stagnant waters, a quarter of a mile away from me in the hollow separated into pools and ponds, by twining reeds and rushes and little knolls of earth.

On the farther bank from me, the trees rose thickly again, and shut out the view and cast their black shadows on the sluggish, shallow water. As I walked down to the lake, I saw that the ground on its farther side was damp and marshy, overgrown with rank grass and dismal willows. The water, which was clear enough on the open sandy side, where the sun shone, looked black and poisonous opposite to me, where it lay deeper under the shade of the spongy banks and the rank overhanging thickets and tangled trees. The frogs were croaking, and the rats were slipping in and out of the shadowy water, like live shadows themselves, as I got nearer to the marshy side of the lake.

I saw here, lying half in and half out of the water, the rotten wreck of an old overturned boat, with a sickly spot of sunlight glimmering through a gap in the trees on its dry surface, and a snake basking in the midst of this spot, fantastically coiled and treacherously still. Far and near, the view suggested the same dreary impression of solitude and decay; and the glorious brightness of the summer sky overhead, seemed only to deepen and harden the gloom and barrenness of the wilderness on which it shone.

I turned and retraced my steps to the high, healthy ground; directing them a little aside from my former path, towards a shabby old wooden shed, which stood on the outer skirt of the fir plantation, and which I had not noticed before.

On approaching the shed, I found that it had once been a boathouse, and that an attempt had been apparently made to convert it afterwards into a sort of rude arbour, by placing inside it a firwood seat, a few stools and a table. I entered the place and sat down for a while, to rest and get my breath again.

I had not been in the boathouse more than a minute, when it struck me that the sound of my own quick breathing was very strangely echoed by something beneath me. I listened intently for a moment and heard a low, thick, sobbing breath that seemed to come from the ground under the seat which I was occupying. My nerves are not easily shaken; but on this occasion, I started to my feet in a fright – called out – received no answer – summoned back my recreant courage and looked under the seat.

1. In what ways is 'Blackwater Lake' an appropriate name for the lake that the narrator comes across? Find at least three references taken from *both* the second and third paragraphs.

2. There are a number of vivid descriptions of trees in the text (for example, the trees at the house itself and the trees on the opposite bank of the lake). How are these trees described, and what atmosphere do they create?

3. Why does the writer introduce the boathouse at a later point in the text rather than at the beginning, before the narrator has walked down to the lake? Think about what we are told *before* the narrator reaches the shed, and about the atmosphere that has been built up.

4. It might be said that the writer describes things as if through a camera lens.

   • Can you find at least one example of a point where he gives us a wide view of the scene, and an example of one where he focuses very carefully on a close-up detail?

   • How do these descriptions contribute to the overall atmosphere created in the text?

5. What *type* or *genre* of text do you think this is? Support your viewpoint with evidence from the text itself, making reference to similar texts if you wish.

The death of handwriting

The death of handwriting impoverishes us

Melanie McDonagh believes keyboards can never reveal the personality of the author

My daughter's birth certificate came as a nasty shock. For as long as I could remember, state certificates in Ireland were filled in by the same class of clerk: people with conscientious, neat handwriting, which bore all the stamp of having been taught by nuns. But the world has changed. My child's certificate was computer generated, and bore no nice signature from the registrar. There was one from me, but as it had originally been written on one of those digital screens that delivery men use, it was an unrecognisable scrawl. So, no personal touch there then.

That's the way things are going. In her soon-to-be-published book, entitled *Script and Scribble: A Defence of Penmanship*, the American author Kitty Burns Florey contends that handwriting is becoming a lost art. By the next generation it will, she says, have gone the way of Nineveh and Tyre: 'There's a widespread belief that, in a digital world, forming letters on paper with a pen is pointless and obsolete... I am part of the last generation for whom handwriting was taught as a vital skill.' She was prompted to write the book when she discovered that handwriting in some schools was being replaced by keyboarding instruction. She concluded that, in the near future, handwriting will only be used by people who keep a diary. 'I suspect,' she says, 'that there are people today who have never received a letter written on paper and mailed in an envelope with a stamp.'

The obvious question is, does it matter? I'm someone who has gone from writing naturally with pen in hand, to now only being able to think fluently in front of a keyboard. If I tried to construct this article on paper, I couldn't do it. When it comes to letters, of course I write them – quite nicely, if I do it with a dip pen and ink – but emails come easier. One reason why older people write letters to newspapers, while young people comment online, is that younger people don't think on to paper any more. And undoubtedly, they are more legible when chasing a flashing cursor across a screen.

There can be no doubt that we are witnessing the creation of the first keyboard generation. Just over two years ago, a US study of 1.5 million 16 and 17 year olds found that only 15 per cent of them used joined-up writing. Most used block capitals – baby writing. Over here, about a third of boys and a quarter of girls don't reach the Government's required standard by the age of 11, and anyway, the National Literacy Strategy doesn't require those that do to use old-fashioned cursive script. And, by God, you can tell.

It is the most significant development since the working class stopped putting crosses instead of signatures, and I'd say it's a dehumanising trend. For a few years, I worked with medieval manuscripts. And although I wasn't much good at **palaeography**, I rather got to love the way one hand would differ from another. There were quirks, little cartoons in margins – including rude ones – funny little fingers drawn on the side identifying passages of interest, flourishes and the signs of haste. There was an immediacy between writer and reader which could make the centuries vanish. And I remember the horrible shock when I moved from manuscript books to early printed ones.

What! No little pictures, no underlinings? Everything the same? Gross.

Well, that's pretty well where we're at if the written word goes out of fashion. We'll still be communicating, but one essential aspect will be absent: the personality that is invested in the writing. **Graphology** may be a dud science, but on an everyday basis our writing does say something about who we are. If we lose one of the three Rs, we'll be the poorer for it.

Melanie McDonagh, *Daily Telegraph*, 27 Feb 2009

1 The writer provides both personal experience and separate factual information as evidence of what has happened to handwriting in recent years. Identify one example of each from different parts of the text.

2 The writer says that the disappearance of handwriting is creating the first 'keyboard generation', and that this is a 'dehumanising trend'. Explain what you think she means by these two phrases, and say whether or not you agree with her.

3 How does the final paragraph sum up the writer's overall viewpoint about handwriting?

4 The writer uses language in different ways to draw the reader into what she is saying. Find and comment on the impact of at least two of the following techniques.

- her use of informal or chatty language

- her use of questions

- her use of short, snappy sentences or phrases after longer, more reflective ones

- her detailed description of handwriting in medieval manuscripts

- her use of personal pronouns such as 'our', 'us' and 'we'.

Glossary

palaeography: the study of handwriting and manuscripts of the past

Graphology: the study of handwriting, especially to analyse the writer's character

The decline of album sales

Album sales are declining, but it's part of the battle between art and commerce

It may seem like the end of days as people download individual tracks. But these changes are what push pop forward

As Robbie Williams scores the 1,000th No 1 album with *Swings Both Ways*, news emerges that the album itself is in terminal decline. In 2013, for the first time in 30 years, there will be no million-album-selling artist in the UK. People are more likely to cherry pick individual tracks from iTunes than to buy the whole thing. For those who still think of albums as complete concepts – from the progression of songs, through to the artwork, the gatefold cover, the poetic sleevenote, the joke in the run-out groove – it may seem like the end of days.

People have a notional memory of the album as a desirable object, yet layers of mystery have been stripped away from it, gradually, for more than 30 years. In 1980, Dexy's Midnight Runners still felt precious enough about their album *Searching for the Young Soul Rebels* to snatch the master tape because apparently they thought the gaps between the songs weren't the right length. Yet for every Dexy's there's a Michael Jackson. *Thriller* may remain the bestselling album of all time, but it stretched the borders of the album itself as seven of its nine tracks were released as singles – was it ever conceived as a thematic album, a record intended to be heard in one sitting, or was it always something to be broken up into radio-friendly bite-sized pieces?

Essentially, the way we hear music has always been driven by the medium. The 33rpm vinyl album was born from second world war military technology. Prior to this the only way to hear recorded music was on shellac 78s with a playing time of three or four minutes, but from 1948 onwards we could listen to music for roughly 20 minutes at a time without having to get up and turn over the record. When the cassette tape became increasingly significant in the 70s and 80s, a vinyl album fitted neatly on to one side of a C90. For these reasons alone, the standard running time for an album became roughly 45 minutes. Music was written and recorded to fit the brief – Genesis's 1972 progressive rock "suite" *Supper's Ready* just happened to be 22 minutes, 54 seconds long, not coincidentally the optimum length for one side of an album.

The advent of the CD meant acts, especially in America, began to release 80-minute-long albums, just to fill the available space and create a feeling of value for money. Traditionalists balked, even though their tradition only stretched back three decades. More recently, the "deluxe" edition has muddied the waters further. If you bought Amy Winehouse's *Back to Black* when it came out in 2006, it must have been galling to see the album re-released a year later with a bonus disc of songs including her biggest hit, 'Valerie'. At this point, CDs were still selling but losing ground to downloads – Winehouse's label didn't seem too fussed about compromising the integrity of her album-length vision to prop up the ailing format with a cheap giveaway. [...]

There's nothing to stop anyone from releasing an album in the "traditional" way – 40 minutes long, with a loose concept to link the songs together. If you don't want people to download the tracks individually there are various ways to make sure they can't: make the album one continuous mix; make it available on physical formats only – vinyl, CD, cassette if you must – for a week or a month before it becomes available to download, ensuring hardcore fans will hear the album as the artist intended it to be heard; or, and here's the option the industry will be least keen on, try a more aggressive pricing policy, make albums cheaper than £9.99, and encourage people to buy the whole thing rather than two or three tracks.

As was the case in the 20s, when jazz was played faster to fit a song on to one side of a 78, technology still dictates how music is recorded and consumed. It's been a long time since albums were seen as 45-minute slices of someone's life. Lady Gaga's *Artpop* may yet emerge as a deluxe edition, or an expanded edition, or as a bottle of perfume with a free memory stick. The battles between art and commerce, between conservatism and progression, are what push pop forward. Don't let it get you down.

Bob Stanley, *The Guardian*, 24 November 2013

---

1 List three facts we learn about album sales from the first paragraph.

2 In the second paragraph, the writer questions the notion that albums in the past were always 'complete concepts'. What example does he use, and how does he describe the tracks on the album? Use an apt quotation to support your answer.

3 Throughout the text, the writer talks about the 'album' in a range of ways. Select three words or phrases he uses and explain what they suggest about the album's 'life', or about how it was viewed in the past and is now seen in the present.

4 Looking at the article as a whole, what do you think the writer's viewpoint is? Find the quotations that express this viewpoint most clearly.

'Aunt Julia' by Norman MacCaig

Aunt Julia

Aunt Julia spoke Gaelic
very loud and very fast.
I could not answer her –
I could not understand her.

She wore men's boots
when she wore any.
– I can see her strong foot,
stained with peat,
paddling with the treadle of the spinning wheel
while her right hand drew yarn
marvellously out of the air.

Hers was the only house
where I've lain at night
in the absolute darkness
of a box bed, listening to
crickets being friendly.

She was buckets
and water flouncing into them.
She was winds pouring wetly
round house-ends.
She was brown eggs, black skirts
and a keeper of threepennybits
in a teapot.

Aunt Julia spoke Gaelic
very loud and very fast.
By the time I had learned
a little, she lay
silenced in the absolute black
of a sandy grave
at Luskentyre.

But I hear her still, welcoming me
with a seagull's voice
across a hundred yards
of peatscrapes and lazybeds
and getting angry, getting angry
with so many questions
unanswered.

1   A number of phrases or lines in the poem suggest that Aunt Julia's house was in a countryside setting rather than a town one. Find at least two examples, and explain why you selected them.

2   Although the poet does not say what age he was when he stayed with his aunt, how does he imply that he was a child? Think about

- the relationship between the poet and his aunt

- the way in which the 'story' of the poem is told

- any other details the poet reveals.

Make sure you refer closely to actual words, lines or phrases from the poem.

3   A number of verses link or repeat ideas and words in the poem. Which verses are linked, and what do you think the effect of this linking is? Consider

- repeated lines or phrases

- linked situations or descriptions.

4   How does the poet use powerful imagery to convey Aunt Julia's physical appearance and movements?

5   Do you think that the poet enjoyed staying at his aunt's? Explain your opinion with close reference to the poem.

6   What evidence is there from the poem that it is set in a particular culture, and in a time different from today? Think about

- dialect words

- references to pastimes or activities

- names of places.

Notes

Teacher Guide

The general aim of these books is the practical and everyday application of **Assessment for Learning**: to ensure every child knows how they are doing and what they need to do to improve. The specific aim is to help every child progress and for you to be able to track that progress.

The books empower the student by modelling the essential skills needed, and by allowing them to practise and then demonstrate independently what they know and can do across every reading and writing strand. They help the teacher by providing opportunities to gather and review secure evidence of day-to-day progress in each strand. Where appropriate (and especially at lower levels) the books facilitate teacher scaffolding of such learning and assessment.

The series offers exercises and examples that we hope will not only help students add descriptive power and nuance to their vocabulary but also expand the grammatical constructions they can access and use: above all, the ability to write and read in sentences (paragraphs, texts) – to think consciously in complete thoughts. We aim at fuller, more complex self-expression – developing students' ability to express themselves simply or with complexity and the sense to choose when each mode of expression is apt.

Each chapter progresses through a series of emphases, to be practised and mastered before bringing it back to the real reading and writing (of whole texts) in which all these – suitably polished – skills can be applied.

The *Aiming for...* series has been extremely popular in schools. This new edition retains all that was successful about the old but has improved it further in several significant ways.

- This book positively tracks progress in the new curriculum, so each chapter has been updated to ensure thorough coverage of the Key Stage 3 Programme of Study and the Grammar, Vocabulary and Punctuation Appendix to the Key Stage 2 Programme of Study.

- The new progress categories of Some/Good/Excellent correspond to the old sublevels of low Level 6, secure Level 6 and high Level 6.

- A matching chart to the new curriculum is available on www.collins.co.uk/aimingfor.

- The 'Applying your skills' section of each topic is now consistently focused on longer writing tasks designed to build the writing stamina and independence needed for GCSE.

We hope you enjoy using the resources.

Gareth Calway and Mike Gould

Series Editors

1 Make relevant points with apt quotations

Getting you thinking
Take feedback from pairs, eliciting particularly effective uses of evidence and showing how students have related them to the point made. Tell students that it can be relatively easy to find ideas, but that putting them on paper in a fluent way can be more challenging.

How does it work?
Go through the model student response carefully with the class. Ask if there are any aspects that could have been embellished or developed further. For example, the student could have added

> The writer also delays the moment at which the race starts by showing how his thoughts were diverted by memories of a play that 'flashed through' his mind. This further builds up the suspense as we wait for the start.

Now you try it
Students should work on their own for this task. You might wish to give them some prompts to get them started. For example:

> Bannister conveys the continuing tension and uncertainty by using...

For Activity 3, ask students to work through the Branson text in pairs. For the first point, they could use references such as 'I came up with a great plan' and 'Pound signs danced in my eyes'; for the second, they could focus on '...were not a success, but I learned from them' and 'Even at an early age I planned long term'.

Apply your skills
The celebrity could be a sports personality, a pop star, a movie star or any other famous person. It could also be a student's personal hero, someone who has an inspiring, lively story to tell.

Students could write up their tips on an A4 sheet and display them around the room. They could then move around the class to look at the different sets of tips, and evaluate which ones are the best to follow.

2 Compare how poems approach similar ideas

Getting you thinking
a) Pupils might say that this is a poem about 'nothing' – and in one sense they are right! Nothing much happens; it is an observation of a lonely scene.

b) The poem's references to food and rubbish suggest that its setting is a town or city. However, it is also set in winter and at night-time.

c) The atmosphere could be said to be weary, with everything seemingly fading or decaying. Images and details that convey this mood are 'withered leaves', 'vacant lots' and 'burnt-out ends of smoky days'. The objects in the poem are described as empty or forlorn; even the leaves have decayed. The air of hopelessness is reinforced by the weather and by direct use of the word 'lonely'.

How does it work?
Go through the model paragraph with students. Draw particular attention to the way the final part extends the idea.

Now you try it
Students might mention

- how the light 'spreads darkly downwards', suggesting a weary, hopeless tone (even the light is dark!)

- that the use of the words 'silence' and 'loneliness' suggests emptiness, a lack of human activity

- the 'empty' chairs and the description of the empty dining-room

- the 'shoeless corridors', which suggest that nobody is around; the porter is still there but he is alone and reading to pass the time – the only things that are full are the ashtrays.

Apply your skills
Students can use a structure like this to plan their ideas:

Introduction	An overview of how the two poems are similar in terms of what they describe
Paragraph 2	How the settings are described and the effect that is created (for example, loneliness, decay, boredom, absence)
Paragraph 3	What the form/structure of each poem is like, and what that adds. (You could comment on the minor sentences and shorter lines in the first poem compared to the fuller statements of the second, or on the effect of the repetition of the same rhyme sound three times in the first poem ('clock/lots/pots'; 'feet/beat/street') with the more regular pairs of the second.)
Paragraph 4	How other people appear or don't appear in each poem
Paragraph 5	Which poem you found most atmospheric or powerful, and why

You may want to help students by working on the second paragraph together as a class, taking ideas from students and then allowing them to complete the remaining paragraphs independently.

3 Understand how a viewpoint is developed

How does it work?
Talk through the guidance on how the headline and sub-heading work. You could draw out how a word such as 'grip' personifies the weather, and also how the viewpoint here is not stated directly but implied by the tone of the language.

Now you try it
The viewpoint is that there is no excuse for the transport authorities not being able to cope. This is made clear by references to how the situation was

- entirely predictable

- not as bad as the Blitz, through which transport was maintained

- avoidable if roads had been gritted and severe weather warnings had been heeded.

The conclusion makes it clear that the writer thinks that transport bosses are particularly to blame for the situation.

Tell students that a newspaper might be politically biased against a certain government. As a result, the newspaper's coverage may be particularly forgiving or unforgiving of apparent mistakes by that government.

Students can work in pairs to complete the table in Activity 3. They should focus on phrases such as 'standstill', 'completely caught out', 'backlash', 'left stranded' and so on. Once the students have completed the table, select one of the quotations and as a class construct a paragraph explaining the writer's viewpoint.

Apply your skills
You could suggest to the class that when writing the letter from the authorities they could use one of the reasons once actually given – that the disruption was caused by 'the wrong kind of snow'!

4 Summarise and synthesise information

Getting you thinking
It might help to photocopy the travel itinerary for students, so they can highlight or underline the relevant sections.

The key pieces of information are: the name of the airport; the fact that they will be met by a rep; and that private transport (not public) has been arranged. It is not vital to know that the terminal is 'spacious and new'.

How does it work?
Elaborate on the points above by adding that while 'spacious' and 'new' are not vital in terms of key travel details, they might be of interest in terms of persuading someone to visit.

Now you try it
Point out that synthesis is an important skill if you have to bring together different elements from one text or more. In the travel itinerary extract, three particular aspects of Marrakech are noted:

- its magnetic qualities: 'magical' and 'intoxicating'

- its age: 'medieval', 'old'

- its impressive buildings: 'famous souks', 'huge…square'.

To synthesise these points, students need to think of words that sum up each of the qualities. In this case, the second example sentence does this well, reducing each of the points into single adjectives: 'charismatic', 'ancient' and 'memorable'.

Apply your skills
You could also ask students to carry out the following extension activities.

- Choose a country or city that interests you. Investigate how the place or city has been described in various types of texts such as travel guides, novels, poetry and travel writing. Do you notice any similarities or differences?

- Consider the area in which you live. How would you describe it if you were trying to sell it as a holiday location? How would this be different if you were describing it in a non-fiction travel writing account?

1 Make inferences from challenging texts

Getting you thinking

The poem implies many things without spelling out any one of them. It is mainly constructed of simple statement sentences (even the 'which' and 'but' clauses at the very end are given a line each to help keep them simple and clear). This suits the simplicity of the bird persona, which arrives early 'simply because [it] heard' it should and 'never ask[s] how long' it should continue waiting. We might also infer the poet is mocking herself insofar as she behaves like this persona.

How does it work?

Students should recognise the irony in the poem, and back up their ideas by quoting from the text. They need to infer the meaning behind the actual given words, which is that the poet's efforts to be well prepared have 'ended in failure.'

Apply your skills

Point out that birds are commonly used as symbols in poetry (and song lyrics). An owl often symbolises wisdom. Can students think of any poems or songs involving a raven, lark, nightingale, cuckoo, dove, robin or any other bird? What does the bird symbolise in each case?

Ask students the following questions.

- Why do you think the poet adopts a persona in the poem?

- What does this choice imply about the narrator? What would you infer about a narrator who adopts the persona of a worm or a rat?

2 Develop interpretations across texts

Now you try it

It might be helpful to photocopy the *Romeo and Juliet* extract in large format so that students can clearly mark in their directions.

Romeo and Juliet's dialogue here is a sonnet. The legendary lovers meet at a party, probably on a dance floor, and their first dialogue is a love poem full of holy words.

Ask students the following questions.

- What is Romeo angling for?

- What is Juliet's initial – and eventual – response?

Romeo and Juliet's love proves fatal to them both at the end of the play. Ask students to look up the words 'pilgrim' and 'shrine' and list all possible meanings. Do they get any hints from these meanings about the 'path of true love' or its fatal end? What do they infer from the word 'shrine' and how might that affect the way we read 'pilgrim', 'saint' and other 'holy' words?

Emphasise that the elevated, emotional language is not just the difference between modern and Elizabethan English. With the sonnet's hushed, breathless tone and extended religious metaphors, Shakespeare has made it prayer-like, as if worshipping the loved ones.

Sophie Hannah's poem (on page 18) uses the opposite of Shakespeare's 'heightened' language but this is precisely what makes the last line so moving.

Apply your skills

When students have completed their answers, they could use them to respond to this question: 'What change is implied in Romeo and Juliet's relationship from the beginning to the end of the extract?' Ask them to write a paragraph, using evidence from the extract.

3 Consider the wider implications of themes, events and ideas in texts

Getting you thinking
Students should note from the text that in Bradford the police are not used to seeing homeless people sleeping rough, so the homeless are moved on and the boy gets no sleep. Also, people hardly ever give money to the homeless.

How does it work?
The boy wants to be inconspicuous and left alone. In Bradford he was 'getting moved on every hour' so he prefers to be homeless in London. This implies that the police in London are desensitised because the problem is so great.

We can deduce that the boy is pretty street-wise. He is realistic about London: he 'knew the streets...weren't paved with gold'. The repetition of 'knew' reinforces this. He is also aware that he will be one of 'thousands...sleeping rough and begging for coppers', not an isolated case. Nevertheless, he believes that London will offer something better – a chance to improve his life.

Now you try it
In Activity 3, students should note that

- London offers a new beginning and new opportunities

- the boy has a 'clean sheet' – nobody knows him

- London is not 'paved with gold'; thousands sleep rough

- Bradford (by implication) is a place where nothing happens; the boy sees the move from there as a chance to change things and to escape/invent his past

- the negative and passive forms of verbs that convey his state of mind.

In Activity 4, students should show awareness of how the active/passive and positive/negative verb forms convey the boy's changing state of mind as he talks about London and Bradford.

4 Explore the connotations of words and images

A good example of an image denoting connoting something different is the famous picture of Che Guevara: it denotes a soldier but it connotes revolution.

How does it work?
Feed back students' answers from Activity 2. Draw out the following points:

- 'Breakfasting' is sinister if you might become the breakfast! The stone ball crushed like a Malteser *denotes* the demolition of this part of the old school gate. The same applies to the drainpipes becoming macaroni (food again). But both connote a world where huge forces are crushing the very structures of the girls' world.

- The threat seems bigger than just having to use the boys' school because the text uses imagery to convey a deeper level of meaning. The menacing machine is forcing them out of their familiar environment and into the unknown, intimidating world of the boys' school.

Now you try it

It would be useful to share the following terms with students as they come to read and analyse the passage.

- *pathetic fallacy*: where something non-human (such as weather or scenery) represents a human emotion, as when a storm accompanies a murder in horror stories

- *transferred epithets*: where a descriptive word is transferred from a human to a non-human object (for example, the hump-backed bridge here cannot feel misery; it is the girls in the marching column who feel miserable).

The mood created is a depressing one. The weather is cold and windy (again using personification), which reinforces the idea that the boys' school will be unwelcoming and possibly hostile. 'Funereal' suggests death and decay, and the 'flaking paint' and 'sagging gates' make the environment seem unloved and gloomy.

5 Explore what can be inferred from the finer details of texts

How does it work?

Explain that a model answer

- analyses information and makes comments on some finer details of the text

- is clear and makes it easy to understand what the student thinks

- shows that the student has read the text carefully, and makes detailed inferences about characters and their relationships

- embeds quotations effectively into different sentences.

For example:

From the beginning of the extract, I infer that Auntie Lynn is very protective of Robin. Near the beginning of the extract, Jan Mark lists the different things that Auntie Lynn has provided for Robin – 'plenty of clothes', 'a spare pair of pyjamas'. Later in the extract, Jan Mark implies that Auntie

Lynn is overprotective of Robin. It says how she won't have pets in case of 'germs' and also mentions how Robin is almost comically overdressed, even in summer. This all suggests that Auntie Lynn is in danger of smothering her son with too much care. The grammar of the text supports these inferences – for example, 'except four years old' is a subordinate clause in a compound sentence as if it is a side issue to the main sentence. But it is the key point.

Apply your skills

Tell students that they should consider what about Robin's upbringing is stated literally and what is implied. Students should prepare a one-minute class presentation on the detailed inferences that they have made about Robin's character.

1 Comment on how successfully writers have opened their stories

Getting you thinking
Ask students to decide which story opening they like best, and why.

How does it work?
The writer of opening A introduces us to an engaging *character* with words like 'slowly rose to his feet' and 'malignant', which suggest that this is someone potentially evil in a powerful position. The *dialogue* that follows helps the writer to show rather than tell, and to create a feeling of observation and immediacy. A *conflict* or problem is suggested, which immediately grabs the reader's attention and arouses interest – what is the crime of which the other character is accused? What will he or she say? What will happen next?

The writer of opening B establishes a *setting* for the reader by referring to City Cemetery. The *genre* is indicated by the choice of location and the words 'haunted' and 'Halloween'. The beginnings of the *plot*

are also made clear, as a boy's disappearance is mentioned. The mystery of this disappearance captures the reader's interest – what happened to the boy, and why?

Now you try it
Allow students to work in pairs. They should take notes and be willing to defend their decisions.

Apply your skills
Students should work out that if we see the story from Detective Whittier's point of view, it is likely that a crime will have been committed and that he will lead an investigation by interviewing witnesses. The story will probably end in an arrest.

If we see the story from Mrs Brenner's point of view, it is likely that she will want to hide something from the detective. It could be that she has murdered her husband and that the reasons for doing so will be explored in the story.

2 Explore how writers structure a whole text

Getting you thinking
This article is taken from the *Mail Online* and is written by a columnist, Sarah Vine. Talk about the way in which a columnist writes about everyday or topical issues, and how he or she includes personal opinion. Ask students what the title might tell us about the writer's attitude to Christmas.

How does it work?
The purpose of the article, as the title suggests, is to put forward the writer's views

about Christmas. The first sentence of the article sets up the traditional stereotypes of Christmas as a magical time, but then undercuts this in the next sentence. The article continues to criticise the way in which the present reality of Christmas falls short of our grand expectations, before concluding that Christmas has lost its religious origins and become a negative occasion.

The article establishes a clear theme by

- using a *headline* that indicates the theme of Christmas

- using the opening *topic sentence* to name the focus of the article

- *reiterating the theme* throughout ('Christmas', 'festive', 'festive fun', 'tradition', 'celebration', 'Christ').

The article builds toward a conclusion by developing ideas and sequencing paragraphs:

- **Start**: *stating* what traditional notions of Christmas are and explaining what Christmas is like for the writer

- **Middle**: *describing* familiar scenes of Christmas in Britain

- **End**: *returning to traditional notions of Christmas* and stating how these differ from the reality of modern-day Christmas in Britain.

The article engages the reader's interest by

- establishing the topic of Christmas (to which everyone can relate) at the start

- using *colloquial* language and a conversational tone ('rip-off' and 'kick off' are examples of conversational language)

- including personal phrases, such as 'In the case of my family', which make the reader feel like a confidant

- using *exaggeration* and *alliteration* to create humour ('ritual humiliation' and 'so-called festive fun' are overstated examples of feelings to which readers can relate)

- including the *first person* to make the start more accessible for readers.

Now you try it
Remind students about topic sentences and ask them to point out the first two in the article.

Allow students to work in pairs. They should be able to

- work out why the writer uses the topic sentences to repeatedly reference the article's central themes

- spot references to time and place, as well as familiar images of Christmas, and comment on how these help to develop the writer's ideas

- identify connectives that create cohesion.

Check students' progress by asking some pairs to report back to the class.

Apply your skills
Students should plan their article using bullet points or a spider diagram, thinking about everything that they have learned in the lesson.

3 Recognise and discuss the effects of a range of structural features in a text

Now you try it
Draw out with students that the main structural features are stage *directions* (including references to music, light and the position and action of characters on stage), *narration* (by the central character) and *juxtaposition* (such as the juxtaposition of the lecture and its disappointment with the flashback to New Year's Eve). All of these features are used to give us a sense of Adrian Mole's character and, in particular, the gap between his imagination and reality.

If necessary, highlight that George Eliot was a woman, writing in a previous century and long dead! This adds to the humour and shows us that Adrian Mole still has much to learn before he becomes an intellectual.

The *stage directions*, written in italics, indicate that *sound* is used before any visual medium. The Mole Overture is a piece of music that repeats throughout the play. Here it immediately establishes a comical *atmosphere*. When Adrian moves *front stage* and addresses the audience directly, the focus is placed firmly on him as the key *character*. The playwright *juxtaposes* the music with the appearance of Adrian Mole in order to set up a link between this music and this key character.

This character is also acting as a *narrator* (like the *chorus* in Ancient Greek theatre). Through his words we learn about him and his ambitions. We get the impression that he is a rather self-involved and pseudo-intellectual character. He also establishes his family *context* and *setting*. It is clear that Adrian has negative feelings towards other characters; he feels disadvantaged by his dull and embarrassing family and wishes for a more intellectual life.

The playwright juxtaposes Adrian's pretensions with the deflated reality of his existence through her stage directions – the lights go up to reveal a flashback, a remembered scene of a New Year's Eve party. The lights expose Adrian to us, not as the wannabe intellectual who opened the play but as an all-too-ordinary teenage boy. This changes our picture of him and helps achieve the playwright's aim of gently mocking his pretensions. We literally see him in a different light…

Apply your skills

Both playwrights create a sense of mood before either character speaks. Bernard Kops does this through his use of darkness and Otto's formal attire, while Sue Townsend does this through her use of music. We gain an impression of solemnity and sadness in Kops's play, which contrasts with the ridiculousness of Townsend's.

While Townsend juxtaposes reality with Adrian's fantasy, Kops contrasts the death and destruction of war (references to 'silence', 'we were all dead', 'slumped and staring') with the music and dancing that follow news of liberation.

Both plays use a narrator who addresses the audience directly. While Otto's tone is sombre and bittersweet, as his freedom came at such a high cost, Adrian's is comical and farcical (although he doesn't realise this himself).

The symbolism of the silence in Kops's play, on the morning of liberation after a time of gunshots and warfare, is poignant and indicative of the peace to come. The singing blackbird symbolises freedom and joy now that the liberators have come, but its colour also suggests mourning and the sadness of Otto's loss. Otto can't imagine that it could have been a nightingale singing, perhaps because that bird is traditionally associated with poetry and beauty rather than with tragedy.

4 Comment on writers' use of narrative structure to shape meaning

Getting you thinking

Students should be made aware that Sade's memories of the past are presented in italics.

How does it work?

Feedback students' ideas. Draw out with students that the author

- shows how confused Sade is feeling by including a flashback to an event earlier in her life, so that when she is being interrogated about events in the video shop she remembers the last time police came to her house in Nigeria

- uses this device of a flashback and the change from past to present tense to show the difference in time between the two events – one ongoing and one remembered; the present tense signals to readers that this is a flashback and it also makes the memory more immediate for them

- makes clear that Sade is afraid because she associates her current experience of the police in London with her previous experience of the police in Nigeria

- provides readers with Sade's backstory, which helps to fill in gaps in plot; in the sentence 'Frozen inside and out' she suggests the way in which time replays itself for Sade.

Now you try it

Explain to students that a saga is a very long story – for example, the entire life-history of a hero. Mini-sagas attempt to suggest a whole story – even a whole life – in 50 words. A lot is suggested by a little, rather than being explained in detail. Mini-sagas should 'expand in your mind like something with water added', as a recent Radio 4 mini-saga competition judge put it.

Sagas tell the history of great heroes, dynasties or great nations. Ask students to consider whether writers who choose a mini-saga narrative structure are trying to elevate the idea of everyday stories of 'little' people, who are perhaps just as complex or heroic in their own way.

5 Compare the organisation and development of a theme through a whole text

Getting you thinking

An Italian sonnet 'turns' at the end of line 8 – the 'volta' – into a reversal of the ideas expressed in the first eight lines. Ask pupils to identify the word or words that signal any such change in line 9.

How does it work?

Explain in discussion with students that the form and structure of this poem contribute to its meaning in many subtle ways.

Draw out the following ideas.

- The rhythm of the sonnet is iambic pentameter, made up of five unstressed and five stressed beats per line – di-dum di-dum di-dum di-dum di-dum, with any variation from this done for effect.

- The choice of sonnet form is appropriate given the themes in this poem: love and death.

- The use of enjambment in the poem perhaps reflects the way in which the poem serves as a journey towards a better understanding of love and death.

- In line 9 Rossetti provides a turn, or volta, with the word 'yet' suggesting a change in direction. She moves from being remembered to being forgotten, before concluding that it is better for her to be forgotten and for her lover to be happy than it is for her to be remembered and her lover to be miserable.

The sentiment expressed in this poem relates to the idea of being at peace with loss. The sounds in the poem reflect this idea as they are made up of soft 's' and 'l' consonants and soothing assonance. This sets the quiet, solemn mood of the poem. The poet also uses repetition to provide a soft hymn-like tone, and the rhyme suggests the idea of unity – concord rather than discord.

Now you try it

Ask students the following questions.

- What do you think the lack of full rhyme – in lines 2 and 4, and perhaps also 5 and 7 – could suggest in this poem?

- What might the sparseness of the language suggest about the nature of the love being described?

- Can you see any similarities between this poem and Rossetti's in terms of the language that the two poets use?

Students can use a table like the one on page 112 to organise their ideas.

Rossetti's poem	Dickinson's poem	Effect
Sonnet form	Four-line stanzas (quatrains)	The sonnet form was used for serious subjects and often love. The sonnet puts forward the poet's ideas about love. The 'Yet' suggests a change in the discussion about lost love. Dickinson's short four-line stanzas indicate how simple and universal an emotion love is.
First person, personal account		
Regular rhyme		
Regular rhythm: iambic pentameter		

Rossetti's poem	Dickinson's poem	Effect
Full rhymes at the end of lines		
Theme of lost love		
Powerful and intense feelings expressed		
Medium-length lines		
Alliteration		
Enjambment		
Repetition		

Draw out in discussion the similarities and differences between Dickinson's poem and Rossetti's, such as

- like Rossetti's poem, Dickinson's poem is written in the first person, which makes it sound like a personal account

- in Dickinson's poem, the lines are short and the entire poem is actually a single sentence; in Rossetti's, the lines are of medium length and are organised into three sentences across the poem

- Dickinson uses alternately rhyming lines – with an alternate rhythm of iambic tetrameter (eight-syllable lines) and iambic trimeter (six-syllable lines), a classical ballad form; Rossetti's poem is a sonnet in iambic pentameter.

Encourage students to think about why the poet has chosen particular structural features, and how they affect the meaning of the poem.

Apply your skills

Encourage quality rather than quantity in the students' comments and explanations. Emphasise the importance of referring to the text and, where relevant, using quotations.

1 Identify and comment on emotive language

Getting you thinking
Model one example of emotive language for students. Point out that they might have chosen 'choirs of wailing shells': choirs would be seen singing peacefully in churches before the war, but in this poem they are associated with instruments of death. Ask students to work in pairs to find other emotive words and phrases.

How does it work?
In the first half of this poem, Owen suggests that war is insane ('demented'): young men are slaughtered 'as cattle'; it is all a 'monstrous' mockery. This is likely to make the reader feel outrage.

Now you try it
- Students should work out that the girls are girlfriends, young wives, or girls from the soldiers' villages.

- Many of the soldiers had no graves. Thousands were killed in one day and their bodies were left in no man's land. The 'patient minds' could be the parents of the dead soldiers; they might be unaware of the death of their sons, or accepting of the fact.

- The parents of the dead soldiers would draw the blinds in respect for their sons.

Apply your skills
Students should work out that, after four years of fighting, Sassoon and the soldiers are feeling elated, relieved and glad that the war has ended. We should 'feel' his happiness. The choice of words might be singing/delight/freedom/beauty. Sassoon also compares his freedom from war with a caged bird that has been set free.

2 Infer and comment on meaning in persuasive texts

Getting you thinking
Point out that Jessie Pope (1868–1941) lived at a time when patriotism was highly regarded as a social virtue, that she did not have – and could not have had – any first-hand experience of battle, and that her pro-war poems reflected widely held views. You could also mention that Wilfred Owen's 'Dulce et Decorum Est' was originally addressed to her.

Draw out that Pope's poem uses positive language that paints a picture of the war as a game that all brave young men should be prepared to play. She suggests that the worst that will happen is that they may 'come back with a crutch'. She says that there is only really 'one course to pursue' (at least for a patriot), implying that to 'lie low' instead is cowardly.

The questions beg an answer, and help to create a positive, enthusiastic tone – rather like 'Anyone for tennis?' The clichés would help to persuade young men that no extraordinary heroism or sacrifice was required – just normal, everyday decency. A colloquial phrase like 'no picnic' would be immediately recognised and appreciated by all.

Now you try it

Churchill's speech is informed by personal experience of battle, and he was attempting to sustain morale in the more obviously valid cause of World War II. However, his language is still carefully chosen for its impact. He uses the power of positive and negative word associations: the phrase 'move forward into broad, sunlit uplands' is clearly positive in all its connotations, just as 'sink into the abyss of a new Dark Age' is entirely negative.

In Activity 7, students should be aware that the pronoun 'him' makes the battle seem more personal. The context is that Churchill was leading a democratically elected government against 'him' – a single Fascist dictator intent on conquest and subjugation.

Apply your skills

In groups, or as the whole class, students could debate how effective each text would have been at the time when it was written.

3 Explain and comment on writers' use of irony

Getting you thinking

It might also be worth mentioning *dramatic irony* here (when an audience knows something the characters in a play do not). You could use an example of dramatic irony from *Macbeth*, in which Duncan and Banquo comment on the healthy air as they approach Macbeth's castle – where Duncan will be murdered.

Harper Lee is not the first author to comment with gentle irony on his or her own childhood perceptions. Mark Twain does this in *Old Times on the Mississippi*, when he recalls being jealous of a boy who got a job on a steamboat, and Laurie Lee also does it in *Cider with Rosie*.

How does it work?

Invite students to think of examples from their own lives of things that they once believed to be true but that were subsequently proved wrong. A further development would be for students to write about these experiences in a similar way to Lee. Essentially, Lee presents Scout's views without ever saying 'Scout/I used to naively think that…'.

Now you try it

Encourage students to notice the following points in particular:

- Swift's tone in phrases such as 'of my acquaintance', 'most delicious, nourishing, and wholesome food' and 'humbly offer it to public consideration'. How formal or informal is this? What attitude to his reader does he seem to have?

- The phrase 'persons of quality and fortune'. What would Swift actually think of wealthy people who ate children?

- What is especially ironic about Swift's suggested advice to mothers, and the words he uses for it?

- The phrase 'plump and fat for a good table'. What does it sound as if Swift is describing? In what sense is the table 'good'?

Apply your skills

It is outlandish to suggest that Irish babies should be eaten. However, A 'Modest Proposal' addresses the fact that something has to be done about Irish poverty. By using irony, Swift brings attention to the serious problem that Ireland faced.

It is worth pointing out to students that some people at the time did not realise Swift was using irony, and thought he really *was* suggesting that Irish babies should be eaten!

4 Analyse how writers use different sentence structures and rhythms

In this lesson, encourage students to 'hear' the rhythms that different sentences create. For example, sentences can be: short and sharp; balanced between two viewpoints; or winding and sinuous, with lots of caveats and subordinate clauses.

Getting you thinking

- Ask students to reflect on their reading of the Elizabeth I speech.

- Do they notice a different kind of pause when a semicolon, as opposed to a comma, is used?

- Which parts of the sentence would they emphasise if they were performing it for real?

- Are there any individual words they would stress?

- Do they think the sentence structures work well in the speech?

- Do they notice any other effective features (such as repetitions building to a climax)?

- Would the speech work better with simpler sentences?

- How does Elizabeth I try to appeal to her army?

How does it work?

Draw out that Elizabeth's long, complex sentences create an impressive sense of her dignity and noble eloquence, yet their phrasing and punctuation (for sense and spoken impact) make them fairly easy to follow. Of course, one wonders how many of her soldiers would actually have been able to hear her words. Those not in the front ranks may have had to rely on a simplified paraphrase of the key points.

Now you try it

Remind students of the definitions of simple, compound and complex sentences.

- **Simple**: a single complete clause containing a subject and a verb. (Example: *He rushed home.*)

- **Compound**: two simple sentences joined with 'and', 'or', 'but' or 'yet'. (Examples: *He rushed home and found his mother asleep. He rushed home but was still late for dinner.*)

- **Complex**: one or more clauses often joined by conjunctions such as 'because', 'however', 'when', 'where', and so on. One clause will be the main clause (*he rushed home*), while the other(s) adds extra information to the sentence and is therefore subordinate to the main clause. (Example: ***Because he was already late***, he rushed home, ***only to find she had already gone***.)

Explain to students that in this passage Orwell uses a combination of simple, compound and complex sentences in a rhythmical way. He often begins a new subject – and a new paragraph – with a short sentence that sets out the subject of the paragraph. In this case, it is 'In January there came bitterly hard weather.' This fact leads to there being a lot of meetings, in which Snowball and Napoleon (two of the pigs in charge) clash.

The next sentence is a little longer. It is a compound sentence, made by joining two short sentences with 'and'. The next sentence, another compound sentence, is longer still.

Then comes a complex sentence with a **subordinate clause**: 'who were manifestly cleverer than the other animals'. (The sentence would work grammatically without this subordinate clause: 'It had come to be accepted [...] that the pigs should decide all questions of farm policy.') Slipping the idea of the pigs' intelligence into the sentence like this cleverly hints at the way in which the pigs themselves have led the other animals to regard them as the natural leaders of the farm.

Apply your skills
The first sentence (simple) and the second (compound) are straightforward, expressing the hard facts of the animals' problems. The long, complex sentence reflects the shifty and manipulative debates of the pigs.

5 Explore different kinds of dialogue in fiction

Getting you thinking
Students can work in pairs or small groups to answer the questions.

How does it work?
This section provides some of the answers to questions in 'Getting you thinking', so ensure that students work properly on the exercise before addressing this section. To comment on how this dialogue is natural but dramatically interesting, students need to see how it suggests character and relationships.

Now you try it
Try to draw out from students that both Jane and her aunt are speaking formally because they are each trying to maintain their dignity in the face of personal insults. Jane, in particular, even aged ten, wants to assume the moral high ground. If she adopted a less formal register, this would lessen the impact of her words.

Apply your skills
Students may find these terms useful when writing their answer: formal, informal, naturalistic, colloquial, dialogue, narrative, telling, showing.

6 Compare how writers use descriptive language in different texts

Now you try it
Go over the answers to the questions with students:

each blade tattooed with tiger-skins (see)	crab-like spiders (see)
chirped/chattered (hear)	growling fatly ... (hear)
rank with dark odours (smell)	

Lee creates humour by seeing things from the point of view of a small boy – the grass is taller than him.

Durrell gives animals human characteristics: ladybirds are 'rotund and amiable', the humming-bird hawk-moths are fussily efficient.

Durrell was a naturalist and gives a closer description of wildlife. Students should find plenty of examples of this.

Apply your skills
Students should work in small groups on the first exercise, or they could individually write down the reasons for their choice and then justify their decisions to the whole group.

This section provides an opportunity for comparison and evaluation. Students should study the actual language of both accounts closely, and then analyse and compare their effectiveness.

1 Use detailed evidence to identify a writer's or an artist's purpose (Part 1)

Getting you thinking

Students should notice that 'the damsel in distress' likes the dragon. She finds him 'nicely physical' with a 'sexy tail'. She does not fancy the boy and she wonders if he has acne, blackheads and/or bad breath. However, she is pragmatic and so goes along with the boy.

The poet is making us rethink assumptions that girls are sweet, passive objects of love and quest, who are bound to submit to their beloved 'rescuer' rather than have their own opinions and feelings. The 'damsel' is not even faithful to the dragon, saying 'a girl's got to think of her future'.

Fanthorpe questions how women are presented in legend and history by giving this girl a surprising voice. Whether the painting is questioning – or promoting – the pale, passive virgin stereotype is a matter of opinion. But the humour comes from subverting the way the painting is usually 'read', which is as a traditional depiction of a damsel in distress.

Now you try it

Medieval knights were nobles in the sense that they were born into upper-class (noble) families, but they were also supposedly 'noble' in the sense of being virtuous and well behaved. Villeins – peasants – were assumed to be 'villains'. Ask students if they think the painter intended his St George to seem noble.

Apply your skills

Students should identify the following points.

- The girl questions whether she wants to be rescued.

- She knows the dragon likes her and she finds him attractive.

- In contrast, she does not fancy her rescuer but she is pragmatic.

- St George appears arrogant, saying 'you couldn't do better than me at the moment.'

- St George asks the girl why she is going against 'sociology and myth' and tells her she has no choice. His will prevails: 'does it matter what you want?'

Students could also complete this extension activity:

Using your quotations and explanations, write three paragraphs arguing that Fanthorpe's purpose is to make the reader rethink traditional ideas about characters and myths. Comment on the language used and on the attitudes of St George and the girl.

For example:

The poet likens St George's horse to a new car he's showing off. In this way, Fanthorpe reduces St George to a vain young man who expects a girl to be impressed by material things.

2 Use detailed evidence to identify a writer's or an artist's purpose (Part 2)

Getting you thinking

Explain to students that this painting is a portrait of Giovanni di Nicolao Arnolfini and his wife Giovanna Cenami, painted by Jan van Eyck. Arnolfini was an affluent merchant living in Bruges in Belgium.

See how many different possible clues students can find in the painting, then ask them to justify their ideas. Allow them to report their findings to the class as a whole.

Now you try it

The artist has included a variety of symbols in the painting that are specific to the period and culture in which van Eyck was painting. In this way, decoding the painting is rather like being a detective, piecing together clues about the scenario he is depicting. A table of 'meanings' for symbols is given in the 'Getting you thinking' section to support students as they investigate and speculate about possible interpretations of the painting. They should understand that no one really knows what the artist was thinking and that their (reasonable) interpretations are valid.

Most art historians think that this picture was painted to show the wedding of this couple (symbolised by them holding hands and by the shoes on the floor), and to wish them blessings (the candle), faithfulness (the dog) and children (the picture of St Margaret and the oranges). The woman in the picture is probably not pregnant: that was just the fashionable 'look' of the time!

Lots of people think the picture in the mirror shows the artist himself. He might have included himself to show he was a friend of the wealthy couple and to add to his status – or he might just have been having fun.

Apply your skills

Help students to realise that artists use details and clues in their paintings to build a picture that conveys their purpose. Writers use words, sentences and paragraphs to build a whole text that fulfils their purpose.

Students can use visual aids (such as PowerPoint or a poster) in their presentation if they wish. Listeners should make sure that they give feedback on the following points.

- Has the speaker looked carefully at the image and come up with his or her own ideas about the artist's purpose?

- Has the speaker given detailed evidence for his or her ideas?

Extension

For homework, students could find a picture that they like and explain what they think it is about.

3 Identify and explain how dramatists create an effect on their audience

Although these pages use an extract from Shakespeare, the ideas are also relevant to other drama texts. Other drama texts often include more stage directions than have survived in Shakespeare's works, and it would be useful to consider the effect of these in formulating directors' choices.

Before you start this topic, ensure that students have a firm grasp of the similarities and differences between plays and films and understand that notions of effect apply to both art forms.

Getting you thinking

The Taming of the Shrew is an interesting play, particularly when read today in such a different context from its own time. Students might benefit from a discussion of: the ethics of paying someone to marry your daughter; Petruchio's attitude to women's talk ('And do you tell me of a woman's tongue'); and the patriarchal values that emerge from this. Shakespeare's repeated use of the word 'I' may suggest that he is not entirely comfortable with Petruchio's character.

If students find it too challenging to read the entire extract, the entire class could read it, with each pair speaking one or two lines. An audio version of the play may also be useful for students, so that they hear the lines read aloud.

How does it work?

As well as Petruchio's repeated use of the personal pronoun, students should consider how his many rhetorical questions make his tone more aggressive – daring the listeners to challenge him and implying that their doubts about his venture are unreasonable.

Apply your skills

Assess students' understanding by listening to their oral interpretations. Partners could swap their written responses with one another to see if they agree about the effects of their chosen tone on the audience's view of Petruchio.

4 Explain the purpose of a text and give detailed evidence to support your points

Getting you thinking

Allow students to work in pairs and then choose a few pairs to report back to the class.

How does it work?

The blurb writer's main purpose is to sell the book – by making it sound comprehensive and reliable. The students need to give detailed evidence for this opinion, finding and explaining words and phrases such as 'first-hand accounts', 'complete guide' and 'expert insights' to support their ideas.

Now you try it

Remind students that the book will be aimed at a wide range of people, not just one type. Students may benefit from working on the table on the right to formalise their ideas from Activity 5 before moving on to the continuous writing task.

Attribute of audience	Textual clue	Reason why they would read this book
Adventurous	The phrase 'festival front line' implies danger and unexplored territory.	To plan new challenges or to make them feel that they could go anywhere.
Like to have information from 'insiders'		

Apply your skills

Students may want to use the following paragraph or sentence starters:

> *The purpose of this text is…*
> *The text targets…*
> *It appeals to this audience by…*
> *This would attract these readers because…*
> *In conclusion, I think that…*

5 Explain writers' viewpoints using detailed textual evidence

Getting you thinking

For Activity 1, students should point out that

- she is a schoolgirl, and wears a blue-and-white uniform
- her hair is golden and she wears plaits
- she looks like a painting
- she has fine sweat on her forehead.

For Activity 2, they should note

- she is young
- she is seen as important/perfect
- she is seen as angelic
- this could be an important moment in the girl's life.

How does it work?

Explain to students that when they are not sure about an author's intentions, they can suggest ideas and phrase interpretations tentatively using phrases such as 'he could be' or 'she may be'. This allows them to express an opinion even if they aren't certain it is correct.

Modal verbs express meanings such as uncertainty, ability or obligation. The main modal verbs are *will, would, can, could, may, might, shall, should, must* and *ought.*

Now you try it

The last line of the poem includes an unusual idea so ask students to look at it closely and think about what it might mean. Why is his hand rather than his mouth 'trembling to recite her name'?

Apply your skills

Ask students if they can work out how the girl feels, using implied meaning from the text. Is she laughing at the boy? Are her companions joining in? Or is she laughing at something else?

You may consider discussing/eliciting poetic features, including

- the positioning of 'Noon' in the first line, which is separated from the following words in order to give sufficient pause and solemnity to the start of the poem
- the use of enjambment in the next section to build up a seamlessly idyllic picture of the girl
- the close positioning of 'singed' and 'signed', and the impact of this on the musicality of the poem
- the use of short, simple sentences on one line to switch between the viewpoints; feelings are revealed in a staccato manner, suggesting raw and tentative emotions, and when the girl returns to her friends the punctuation signals a change in emotion
- the use of personal pronouns to guide the reader's perspective.

6 Understand a text's effect on the reader and explain how the writer has created it

Getting you thinking

Allow students time to read the poem several times.

You could ask students to try the following activities.

a) Examine the collection of images that you have created. What impression does this picture give you of the place that Walcott is describing?

b) In the first seven lines, what picture is created of Tobago in the middle of summer? Is it

- hectic or slow-paced
- crowded or spacious
- lively or sleepy
- rapidly changing
- something else?

c) Now think about how the poet has used punctuation in these lines.

To develop an active response to reading and the use of punctuation in the poem, you could also ask students to do the following activity.

Stand up with a copy of the poem in your hands. Start reading the poem aloud. If you have lots of space, walk in a straight line while you read it. Every time there is a punctuation mark, turn 90°. Always turn in the same direction. When you have read up to 'August', stop and do the whole thing again.

Here is a sample answer to the Activity 3 question 'What do these images tell you about the place that Walcott is describing?'

The poet describes 'sun-stoned beaches' which suggests that in Tobago in midsummer it is very hot. The stones would be hard to touch and the intense sun would make the stones appear white.

The poet then uses colour as a contrast. The heat appears 'white', possibly through the glare of the sun. As a contrast, the river is 'green'. Green is a colour that suggests shade.

The palms in midsummer are 'yellow', like the sun's colour. They are also 'scorched', which means burnt and discoloured. This image suggests the place is so hot that the 'green' has gone from the palms.

In this hot weather, people sleep in summer houses. Here it is impossible to work in the hottest months. People are 'drowsing through August'.

The short, heavily end-stopped lines make the pace of the poem similarly slow and intense.

This response could be used as a 'crib' for teacher modelling of a written answer.

This is a good poem to exemplify to students that a range of responses are encouraged when analysing writing.

Apply your skills

The tone of the poem changes at the end, and the images created at this point are ones of regret. The poet has lived through days in Tobago – 'days I have lost' and has also changed – 'days that outgrow'.

The poet compares the past to daughters he once held in his 'harbouring arms'.

It is an interesting and unusual comparison. The poem therefore seems to be about a place where Walcott once spent his time. He vividly remembers Tobago in midsummer, and he appears to regret that those hot days are past and that they will never return. They are 'lost.'

Remind students that poets often write from a *first-person* point of view, as if they are talking about their own feelings. However, we shouldn't assume that the narrator is the poet. Sometimes poets write from the point of view of a character in the first person and it is the character speaking, not the poet.

Development of the role of the persona in this poem would form a useful guided session for more able students.

1 Recognise textual conventions

Getting you thinking

Equiano's *Interesting Narrative* is – in style at least – like a typical 18th-century autobiography, with a highly conventional 'English-literary' opening: 'I believe it is difficult for those who publish their own memoirs to escape the imputation of vanity…'

This extract is taken from the middle of Chapter 3. Students should work out the unusual way in which snow is mistaken for salt.

Now you try it

Explain that West Indians were raised to regard Britain as their mother country, and that many fought for Britain in World War II. When Britain needed workers, the government offered people a passage from Jamaica on a ship called the *Windrush*. However, the racist reception these Jamaican people received from the British shocked them, and many experienced loneliness and isolation in their new life.

Equiano writes in Standard English; Selvon in a hybrid of Standard English and Creole. This reflects their purposes. Equiano dressed, spoke and wrote like an English gentleman to reinforce his message that Africans were civilised human beings. Selvon is capturing the feelings of his West Indian characters in their own (spoken) idiom, but said that he needed written Standard English to narrate the story.

In the extract by Selvon, key elements of the vocabulary and grammar – for example, the use of present tense to describe the past – are Creole language features. The names – Sir Galahad meeting Moses – add to the strangeness that the dialect creates for a reader of Standard English.

The sentences of both extracts are long and heavily punctuated with commas. The first extract is based on complex sentences; the second on compound sentences.

2 Recognise how textual conventions can be combined to create a new literary form

Getting you thinking

Ask students to discuss the question in pairs.

How does it work?

Show students how in news reporting or historical writing, the same 'story' would be told in other ways. Here are some examples to share with the class.

News: *The famous painting was removed at midnight on Sunday, and taken away for forensic examination by the police…*

History: *Duke Ferrara and his predecessors ruled for 900 years, establishing themselves as one of the most powerful Italian families, bringing to mind the Medici or Borgia dynasties.*

A newspaper article would also have a headline about the murder and the wh- questions – who, when, where, what happened.

This extract, by contrast, is the narrative of a made-up person – a *character* – but arranged so that we see and understand more than he realises. It is literature.

Now you try it

One way of understanding the form is to say that it develops Shakespeare's soliloquies – where his characters 'think out loud' (the verse imitates the speaker's voice patterns) – into a mini-play with a story, character interplay and action of its own.

Apply your skills

Encourage students to understand what *dramatic monologue* means.

- The narrative is told to us in the present (as in a piece of drama).

- Only one character speaks, so it is a monologue. The reader's experience is a bit like hearing one side of a phone call, where you have to imagine what the person on the other end is saying and doing.

3 Discuss how ideas are treated differently in different times and places

Getting you thinking

Encourage students to research how William Wilberforce campaigned to end the slave trade in Britain.

Now you try it

Ask students whether they know where – or how – their clothes were made. Explain that wherever their clothes were bought, lots of our clothing is made in developing-world sweatshops by low-paid (near-slave) workers, often women or very young children. We don't often think about the lives of these workers. Instead, we think of how cool – or uncool – the clothes are, or how cleverly we got them at a bargain price in a 'sale'.

Students interested in this topic might enjoy reading *Iqbal* by Francesco D'Adamo. This book tells the real-life story of Iqbal

Masih, a former child slave who campaigned against child labour in Pakistan until his assassination in 1995. It is believed he was murdered by those hostile to his work for the Bonded Labour Liberation Front.

Apply your skills

Students should work out that attitudes to texts change over time because different societies' values and attitudes are not constant.

There may be a variety of answers from the students. However, ask students if they think texts from previous times should be read today so that we can understand history better and learn from it. Reading texts from previous times should give us a better understanding of where we came from and who we are today.

4 Discuss how texts are interpreted differently in different times and places

Getting you thinking

To begin with, ask students if they know the story of *Frankenstein*. Have they read the novel or seen a film version? Do they have an image in their minds of the creature? If so, where does that picture come from?

Shelley's original version has been interpreted in different ways over the years. In particular, film versions overlooked the monster's own point of view.

How does it work?

Draw out that in a novel the narrator tells us how to 'read' the characters and events. In some novels this perspective is more neutral than others, but it is there in the very act of narrating a story. Importantly, Shelley uses a variety of perspectives in the novel, which reveal information about different characters.

Now you try it

Draw out that in Dear's play, Frankenstein's perspective is still presented but so is the monster's. In fact, Dear's text is intended to be a corrective to the 'monstrous' representations of the film versions, and marks a return to the dilemmas that Shelley originally raised in her novel.

However, a modern text is less likely to demonise 'outsiders' as 'freaks' than a text from 1818. The genre (a play) and modernity of Dear's text bring the monster closer and make us 'read' the story differently from the way Shelley's original readers would have. While Shelley's text was infinitely more sympathetic to the monster than a 'rational' 18th-century text would have been, this modern production is still more so.

Apply your skills

You might want to direct students to the video on the National Theatre website in which Nick Dear talks about updating *Frankenstein* for the stage: www.nationaltheatre.org.uk/search/site/Frankenstein

5 Discuss how the same literary form is used differently in different times

Getting you thinking

Ask students: would they rather have a sonnet written in a Valentine's card – or a limerick? Why? Explain that limericks are traditionally joke poems, usually rude. If you're serious about love, you wouldn't send a limerick. You'd send a sonnet.

Ask students to look at the use of rhyme and punctuation in the poem. Do they notice any patterns marked by strong punctuation? Consider how lines 5–8 and 9–12 repeat the ideas of lines 1–4 in a different way, and how lines 13–14 reverse them. What are these ideas?

Explain to students that before Shakespeare the *convention* was that a sonnet divided at the end of line 8, reversing the idea of the previous lines at the 'volta' or turn. For Petrarch this might mean eight lines of complaining about the way his lady-love – or 'deer/hart' – treats him, then six lines saying it is worth it because of her perfect beauty. Shakespeare is developing the conventions of the English sonnet, partly because it is more difficult to find multiple rhymes in English than in Italian. Notice also how Shakespeare challenges that 'sonnet' convention of perfect beauty.

How does it work?

Remind students that writers rarely invent completely new literary forms. Even Petrarch based his sonnet on a Persian love poem called a ghazal.

Ask students to have a go at writing a 14-line sonnet. This would make a good homework task.

Notes

Notes

Notes

Notes